The Happy Well-Fed Artist:

How to Get Your Creative Project Off the Ground and Into the World

by
Katie Curtin

The Happy Well-Fed Artist:

How to Get Your Creative Project Off the Ground and Into the World

Cover Design: Wendy Wood

Author Photograph: Roy Dudley

Library of Congress Cataloging-in-Publication Data

Curtin, Katie

The Happy Well-Fed Artist: How to Get Your Creative Project Off the Ground and Into the World

ISBN-13: 978-1511441728

ISBN-10: 1511441720

Library of Congress Control Number: 2015908480

BISAC Category: Self Help / Creativity

CreateSpace Independent Publishing Platform, North Charleston, SC

First Printing, 2015

Praise From Happy Readers

Finally, a book to be read and reread by anyone with an artistic spirit! Katie Curtin's book, The Happy Well-Fed Artist, *speaks to the heart of the artist, those people of all artist tastes, flavors, visions and courageous expressions, as directly as an arrow piercing the bull's eye of creativity. Katie does this in a language that is plain-spoken, clear and easily understood. This book addresses many points and guides the risk taker to rid themselves of preconceived negative notions and will help people find "purpose and meaning" in life through their artistic journey. This book and its encouraging, positive first-person advice will allow the reader to feel assured that their efforts are vital to themselves and ultimately, society. Reading* The Happy Well-Fed Artist *is joining Katie on an artistic adventure of life!*

- Honey Novick, Award Winning Singer/Songwriter, Poet and Vocal Coach, www.honeynovick.com

Katie's book shows us that no one has to choose between creativity and earning a living: you can do both and balance them well. She busts the "starving artist" myth and shows you it's not an "either/or" game to fit creative expression into your life – you need to make time for it just like you do eating or sleeping if you want to stay healthy and feel alive. As someone who marries her professional life (marketing and brand consultant) with her creative outlets (acting and writing), I know it can be done and it makes me a better, more innovative professional to boot. Katie gives you the tools and advice to live a more expressive, creative and fulfilled life - whether you choose to be a full-time or "part-time" artist.

- Maria Ross, Founder and Chief Marketing Strategist, Red Slice, www.red-slice.com

I highly recommend Katie's book, The Happy Well-Fed Artist, *to anyone who has ever had, or wishes they had, the 'creative urge.' Katie sparks the desire to make something original without regard for what others expect, just for the joy of the satisfaction of sharing our creative energy. Her book is complete and comprehensive, from myths to manifestation, from the thought of what to make and how*

to do it through the production, PR and possible venues. Once you have read her ideas, there is no reason or excuse to delay in the creation of your own masterpiece, be it mask making, writing, art, puppetry, theatre, or any media at all, as Katie has experienced them all and will show you how. As another renaissance soul, I will treasure this book and return to it frequently for inspiration and practical ideas about the process of making and sharing art.
- Judith Fine-Sarchielli, Iconic Renaissance Woman, Author, Designer and Gluten-Free/PALEO, Tuscan-style chef, www.talesofaglutenfreegypsy.com

I delved into this book with curiosity and discovered a beautifully woven book with inspiring chapters for artists of all ages and forms – visual artists, singers, actors and writers, etc. In this one-of-a-kind book, Katie helps you get out of your own limiting beliefs about what it means to be an artist. Through her own personal stories, she makes you understand that you don't have to beat yourself up just because you are able to paint only once a week – because you might be busy with a full time job or young children.

It is a very easy-to-read book and I found I could relate to almost everything: Should I narrow my focus as an artist and concentrate on one medium only? Should I spend time only painting and not "waste" time taking salsa lessons or voice lessons? Should I spend time only practicing being a life coach? I love all of it and Katie showed me that by allowing myself to do other things, whether they are in the field of art or not, I can come back to what moves me at any given time in life without feeling guilty! This is a really well-written book that is a must for anyone wanting to find different ways to get inspired, stay inspired and in action, deal with distractions, complete a project and show it to the world. Most importantly, it tells you how to handle your "gremlin," that little voice which whispers in your ears, "You can't do it."
- Vanaja Ghose, Artist and Life Coach, www.vanajaghose.com

As a fellow artist and designer, I so appreciate the wisdom that Katie Curtin offers to empower anyone who struggles with believing in themselves, their work and the importance of being paid well for their creative endeavors. She offers very grounded and practical advice to artists on how they can truly make their work come alive and be complete.

Katie clearly understands the challenges that artists go through because she has been there herself. She has very practical advice on how to break through the blocks that hold creative expression back. The Happy Well Fed Artist *is a must-read book for anyone who struggles with giving validity to their creative work. Katie offers a simple step-by-step process that takes one from beginning a creative endeavor all the way to completion. Not only is this a book filled with resources, it is delightful and beautifully written in a way that is most inspiring!*

- Judy K. Katz, MCC, RScP, Author of *Beyond Your Shadows of Doubt*, Artist and Life Coach, www.wealthtransformations.com

Katie's writing style is warm and conversational, while addressing powerful issues on the fears and joys of creativity. She provides healthy, simple ways to promote my artistry.

- Grace Heer, Life Coach and Artist

Katie Curtin has walked the walk of the artist and now she talks the talk of wisdom and the practicality of how to 'make it all work' as an artist in a lived-life. Anyone who has had a longing to be more creative or to delve more deeply into already developed artistic expression will be delighted to read The Happy Well-Fed Artist. It dispels all the negative myths about artists and replaces them with accurate and lively images of artists doing their work and living quite well. Informative, practical and inspiring!"

- Sarah O'Doherty, M.Ed, Educator, www.proceedthroughhighschool.com

I highly recommend Katie Curtin's book, The Happy Well-Fed Artist*! I too am an artist, photographer, coach and performer. I am inspired by Katie's stories and extensive personal experience in the creative arts. I especially loved the Sorrowkeeper story and the Bali adventure. Thank you Katie for your insight, wisdom, encouragement and heart.*

- Becca Pronchick, Chief Relaxation Officer, Permission To Relax, www.permissiontorelax.com

About Katie

Katie Curtin, CPCC, is a theatre artist and coach. She loves to help artists, innovators and change makers who want to move past the obstacles that hold them back from expressing their brilliance so they can get their creative and innovative projects out in the world.

As a modern renaissance woman, Katie has had a colorful and adventurous life. In her early thirties, she quit her steady job working in diesel mechanics. She took her pension fund, enrolled in art classes and later, took a year to travel in Asia and Australia, apprenticing in mask making in Bali, Indonesia.

Since then, Katie has brought joy and creativity into people's lives, through theatre, mask and puppet making, teaching hundreds of arts workshops and classes across Canada and internationally.

A rebel with many causes, she has done what she can to foster social justice and human rights. Katie had been a proud feminist since she first led a battle in her high school for girls to have the right to wear jeans as well as the boys.

Her book, *Women In China*, published at the age of 24, was translated into French and Swedish, as well as being featured in the *Readers Digest International*.

Katie has developed a unique form of theatrical and healing "rants," which she performs at a wide variety of venues, on topics that range from the deeply personal, to the social and political.

She's the founder and co-host of the online Creativity Café, which features discussions with innovators and artists about creativity and change-making.

Katie had her first and only child right before she turned 46 and currently spends her time with family and friends between Canada and Mexico.

You can find out more about Katie at http://www.katiecurtin.com and the Creativity Café at http://www.creativitycafeonline.com.

Dedication

This book is dedicated to the family of artists who I grew up with, my mother, Isabel, my father, Walter and my brothers and sisters, Joe, John, Mary, Caroline and Philippa. The creativity and the love for the arts that you all have, has been a source of inspiration to me and forms the bedrock of this book.

To my husband, Eduardo, whose considerable creative gifts are a source of delight. To my one and only child, Tonatiuh, named after the Aztec God of the Sun, who is the sunshine of my life.

To Maxine Sidran, August Tarrier and Anne Cleveland, who edited this book at different stages and Wendy Wood, who designed the cover and all the others who gave their help, feedback and support along the way.

To Michelle Tocher, whose pioneering work in bringing alive the ancient wisdom of fairy tales along with her mentorship and loving support, has allowed my creativity to go places I never imagined.

To the artists of "The Well," who've allowed me, over the years, to experiment and extend my artistic boundaries within the container of a safe, loving group, you serve as a source of support and wonder.

To all my other artist mentors, teachers, colleagues and friends, as well as those who I have had the pleasure to teach and to coach, you are too numerous to mention, but you nevertheless are very much right here in my heart.

To Claudia Bernardi and América Vaquerano and the Perquin School of Arts, El Salvador, I see in you an inspiring example of art's transformative role. Your work in creating community murals and art helps heal the trauma and the enormous grief and suffering caused by the civil war. You show the potent power of art married with social conscience to be an agent of peace and community healing.

To the artists of the world, past and present, who bring immeasurable richness to our cultures.

To the creative spirit and talents in all of us, which deserve to be nurtured and treasured as the precious jewels of our existence.

Finally and most importantly, this book is dedicated to you, the reader, wherever you are in your journey into the arts, wishing that this book might become a well-used creative resource.

Table of Contents

Introduction

"Don't ask what the world needs. Rather ask – what makes you come alive? Then go and do it! Because what the world needs is people who have come alive."

- Howard Thurman

Creativity is a central source of meaning in our lives... [and] when we are involved in it, we feel that we are living more fully than during the rest of life.

- Mihaly Csikszentmihalyi

Have you ever been faced with a decision that will change the course of your life?

A decision that your heart and soul are calling you to make, one that would force you to break with everything you previously thought was important?

In my late twenties, I was faced with such a decision. Art was calling me and I found it increasingly impossible to ignore its call.

At the time, I was working in diesel mechanics at the Point St. Charles railway shops in Montreal for the Canadian National Railway (CNR). I had fought hard for my job, against prejudice and the belief that women couldn't do such work. With six other women, I had won a highly publicized human rights case against the railways, forcing them to hire women into the trades.

It had been exhilarating to win that battle and show that women were capable of doing such work. I had job security, a free rail pass that allowed me to travel the country as I wished and enough money to support me with a modest lifestyle.

I was making a difference, both on the job and in other activist causes. Yet, at a certain point, I no longer felt the same energy to fight the causes I had been fighting since I was a teenager. After six years of working in the railways, I battled with depression as I dragged myself to work each day.

On the job, breathing in the acrid smells of diesel fuel and Varsol, I daydreamed of building sculptures while welding and created musical theatre scenes in my head while working on the lathe.

Nevertheless, it was no easy decision to leave the job. Could I even survive as an artist? Did I have any real talent and creativity?

Didn't I have a responsibility to my activist causes and to staying in a job I had fought so hard to get? Shouldn't I wait until I retired to do my art? Did the world really need more artists? How could that in any way be of help with our planet in such dire need of transformation?

While I was still working, I began to take courses in painting, drawing and printmaking at the local university and art institute.

Finally, I plucked up all my determination and courage and quit my job to begin my life as an artist.

I used the $5,000, which had accumulated in my pension funds to later buy a ticket to Asia. With the remaining money, I spent a year exploring other cultures, including a two-month apprenticeship in mask making in Bali, Indonesia.

My creative journey since then has taken many twists and turns. There have been many years chockfull of artistic work and others where I've focused more on developing other talents and interests, allowing me to bring in income from many different sources. Raising my son and family responsibilities have also shaped the time I've had for my creative endeavors, particularly in his early years. Through it all, I've never regretted my decision to follow my artistic soul.

Since quitting my railway job, I have created hundreds of masks, built giant puppets and participated in almost every aspect of theatre: writing plays, acting, directing, as well as designing and making costumes, sets and props. I have also developed my very own form of improvisation, which I call "artist rants." These rants, which I perform at a wide variety of venues, cover topics that range from the deeply personal, to the social and political.

I've taught thousands of adults and children in workshops and courses on masks, theatre and creativity, across Canada and internationally. As well, for over ten years, I've coached hundreds of creative souls to cultivate their passion for the arts and get their projects out into the world and thrive.

A Creative and Abundant Life: Yours for the Making
The intention of this book is to bring you the lessons I have learned from my journey, unraveling the tangle of cultural myths and my own disempowering beliefs about what it means to be an artist, navigating my way in a culture that gives little more than lip service

to the arts and is often downright discouraging.

It aims to give you the benefits of my experience and that of other artists, so that you don't have to spend precious years getting through problems that, with the right approach, techniques and tools, can be overcome more quickly.

I am not going to promise you that there is a magic formula whereby art gets created without any effort on your part, without attention to your craft or hard work. But I will promise you that even the hard work and effort can be pleasurable, once you've put aside the self-disparaging comments about your creativity and have placed yourself outside the box of limiting cultural paradigms and beliefs.

I am not going to promise you "get rich quick" schemes, or that by simply following your passion, the money will follow. But I can promise you that there are ways to do your art and your creative projects without going broke. You just have to be as creative about income development as you are in your artistic pursuits. Here, too, I will give you techniques and methods that will assist you in cutting the learning curve and help you to live a rich, creative life in all aspects.

A large part of this book will walk you through the process of doing a creative project and taking it out into the world. Whether you are at the beginning stages of cultivating creativity or you are an artist with many years of experience, it is my hope that you will find inspiration and wisdom that will help you realize more fully your artistic gifts.

I also have a bigger purpose in writing this book, one that speaks not only to my artist dreams but also to my bigger dreams about humanity and planetary transformation.

In our culture, we've lost track of the transformative and soul nourishing power of the arts, they have become a kind of "spectator sport" of superficial entertainment for the masses, often espousing some of the worst values of contemporary culture, whether it be rampant violence and consumerism, or the objectification of women and the perpetuation of sexist and racist stereotypes.

Art can be, instead, a potent tool for building community, for transforming grief and trauma, a way to communicate both spiritual and social-political truths and to espouse values of love, inclusiveness and diversity. It can galvanize people to take action, inspiring them to throw off apathy and despair.

Mallika Sarabhai in her Ted Talk *"Dance to Change the World"* says:

"If we think we can all agree that we need a better world, a more just world, why is it that we are not using the one language that has consistently showed us that we can break down barriers that we can reach people? What I need to say to the planners of the world, the governments, the strategists is, you have treated the arts as the cherry on the cake. It needs to be the yeast."

A powerful example of art as a tool for social transformation can be found in the soul-searing words of poet and activist, Drew Dellinger in *"Hieroglyphic Stairway."*

"It's 3:23 in the morning/and I'm awake/because my great great grandchildren/won't let me sleep/my great great grandchildren ask me in dreams/what did you do while the planet was plundered?/what did you do when the earth was unraveling?...what did you do/once/you/knew?"[i]

This poem has been called "an iconic work of art for the ecology and social justice movements" and his poems have been cited in venues ranging from prison workshops to climate change hearings before the US Congress.[ii]

I believe that when each of us moves beyond the stereotypes and steps courageously into our creative talents, we not only give ourselves an immense sense of pleasure and purpose, but we also bring more light, joy and wisdom to this planet in these challenging times.

I was inspired to create this book, to help others to get beyond the cultural myths that have discouraged many an artist from following their true passion in life.

This book will help you as an artist to discover and remove blocks or beliefs about what it means to be an artist, so that you can prosper and reap the rewards of your gifts as an artistic soul.

Please enjoy the following pages, where you'll be guided on a journey deep into your artistic self. At the end of each chapter, you will find a variety of questions, exercises and action steps that will help you transform any limiting beliefs that have been holding you back from bringing your gifts out into the world.

The world needs you to stand for the true value of art as a medium for all of us to become more deeply connected with ourselves and to the world around us and as a tool to create more joy, beauty and meaning even in the darkest of times.

Setting Yourself Up For Success
This book is here to help you transform any negative beliefs and work habits that might be getting in your way so that you can inspire the world with your gifts. So it's best if you take the time to set yourself up for success. Use the questions, exercises and action steps as a spark to get you started. If you are inspired, please feel free to go beyond what I have given you here to get even more clarity and deepen your experience.

To get the most out of this handbook, I recommend the following:

1. Get an overview of the book

2. Dedicate a quiet space to read and work on the exercises

3. Decide on a time that will work for you to journal

4. Gather the tools that will work for you to journal

    - A book for journaling
    - Your favorite writing tool
    - A warm or cool beverage

Chapter 1: What's Holding You Back: Myths and Artist Stereotypes that Stifle Your Creativity

"We are all creative, but by the time we are three or four years old, someone has knocked the creativity out of us. Some people shut up the kids who start to tell stories. Kids dance in their cribs, but someone will insist they sit still. By the time the creative people are ten or twelve, they want to be like everyone else."

- Maya Angelou

So what is holding you back? Are you telling yourself that you just don't have the time or money? Are you afraid you will fail and be subject to criticism and public humiliation?

Or you have an image in your head about what an artist is supposed to be like and you don't come anywhere close?

Let's look at some of the predominant cultural myths that may be running your artistic life. The very act of questioning the truth of these myths is an important step in setting you free to live a more fully creative life.

Myth #1: To be an Artist You Have to be Poor and Starving

How many people think of artists as happy, well-off people who eat plentifully and live abundant lives? How many times have you heard the phrase about "the starving artist?"

You probably know at least a few artists who have had a difficult time scraping by. Although most manage to put food on the table, many artists' lifestyle can be far from affluent. Certainly it's not easy to make a good living in the arts and oftentimes economic security can be elusive. Being an artist is not like becoming a doctor, or a lawyer or some other professional where there's a clear path to a decent income.

Truth: You Have More Opportunities Than Ever to be an Abundant Artist

Even though there isn't any question that there are plenty of artists with money problems and little economic security, that's only one part of the story. There are also artists who have attained dazzling levels of wealth. In fact, you can argue that far from dooming you to poverty and destitution, being creative can be a gateway to financial ease. Look at the famous actors and musicians you know.

But it's not just the fortunate few superstars who are doing well. In fact, it seems that the poor starving artist stereotype simply isn't true. A 2011 U.S. survey of more than 13,000 alumni of 154 different arts programs showed that pursuing a career in the arts is not "a likely ticket to a life of perennial unhappiness, hunger and unemployment." But the opposite appears to be true "graduates of arts programs are likely to find jobs and satisfaction, even if they won't necessarily get wealthy in the process." [iii]

An article titled, "Study Reveals Artists Have High Salaries" in the Huffington Post (January 11, 2011) cites another study that showed similar findings:

"There was a time when becoming an artist meant devoting yourself to a starving, bohemian lifestyle, sleeping on a futon and burning your rejected works to stay warm. But artists should feel a little more encouraged now that a new study from the National Endowment for the Arts reveals that the artist lifestyle isn't as conventional wisdom might have it.

The recent study was conducted using the 2.1 million artists in the US, comprising 1.4% of the total workforce. The NEA "analyzed 11 distinct artist occupations: actors, announcers, architects, dancers and choreographers, designers, fine artists, art directors and animators, musicians, other entertainers, photographers, producers and directors and writers and authors." They collected data from 2005-2009 and what they found paints the artist's dream as a surprisingly cozy reality.

The median salary for artists is $43,000, compared to the $39,000 averaged labor force as a whole. (Professionals, however, average $54,000.) Within the subdivisions of artists, architects come out the wealthiest—averaging around $63,000—while 'other entertainers' bring up the rear with $25,000. Women are earning $0.81 to the men's dollar, a whole penny more than the general workforce's $0.80 to the dollar. Furthermore, 6 in 10 artists have college degrees, compared with 1 in 3 overall."

With the shifts in the global economy and the expansion of the Internet, creativity is, in many cases, a prerequisite to success and huge new openings are being presented to artists and creative types to live lives more in line with their abilities and dreams.

[7]

Many artists are setting up their own creative businesses and taking advantage of the new possibilities offered by the Internet and online commerce. This gives them the freedom to set their own hours and work at what they love.

Like any entrepreneurial venture, it takes time, hard work and business "savvy" to become successful. You have to know your audience or customers and find the sweet spot between what you create with your artistic talents and what people will pay for.

Often, it is wise to start such a business as a part-time venture, supplementing your income with other sources until it becomes fully viable. Also, you may find that being an entrepreneur is just not for you, or that you prefer a job rather than going it on your own.

Although a discussion of all the different career paths in the arts is outside the scope of this book, there are many excellent offline and online resources where you can explore the options in your field.

You can visit your local library or employment center, browse the resources available and consult with the staff. Or within minutes, you can access information online on art forms, careers, or creative businesses that interest you. At your fingertips are thousands of articles, blogs and forums on any creative subject you could imagine. Social media also gives you unprecedented opportunities to brainstorm, network and share with artists in all fields.

Chapter 6, "Finding the Money: Getting Creative About Funding Your Arts Projects," discusses options for funding your artistic projects, whether you work full or part-time doing other work, or are a full time artist, freelancer, or creative entrepreneur.

So instead of thinking that art dooms you to poverty, start thinking of creative ways that you can make a good living and do your art. And remember that a rich life is available to you at a far smaller price tag than our society would have us think.

A roof over your head, good food on the table, beautiful artwork around you and sweet friends and family go a long way to sustain a person. Add to that music, dancing and singing, along with contributing both to local and world communities and you have an abundant, rich life, full of meaning and purpose.

Myth #2: To Create Great Art, You Have to be Tormented
The image of an artist's mental stability is less than pristine. It's often assumed that the greater sensitivity that many artists display

means that they are doomed to a life of unhappiness.

Just think of Van Gogh, one of the world's most powerful artists and the self-portrait of his anguished face, with one ear cut off, or Frida Kahlo, whose self-portraits cry forth her emotional and physical pain.

Or think of Sylvia Plath, the brilliant poet and writer, whose unhappiness led her to commit suicide at the age of thirty by sticking her head in a gas oven.

Added to that are the constant stories in the media of the unhappy love affairs and addictions of famous actors and actresses. And don't forget all the musicians, writers and other artists who have drunk or drugged themselves to death.

A BBC news article in October 2012 reported on a Swedish study by the Karolinska Institute, of one million people, that showed that writers had a higher risk of anxiety and bipolar disorders, schizophrenia, unipolar depression and substance abuse. They were almost twice as likely as the general population to kill themselves. Dancers and photographers were also more likely to have bipolar disorder.

Truth: Creating Art Can be an Enormous Source of Happiness and Well-Being

Medical studies have shown a higher percentage of bipolar and depressive disorders among some groups of artists. However, as a group, those in the creative professions were no more likely to suffer from psychiatric disorders than other people.

Art in itself is not the cause of the unhappiness—in fact it's quite the opposite.

One of the most wonderful things about art is that it allows us to create works of beauty out of our greatest sources of suffering. Art has allowed me to find the path out of dark times.

This was particularly the case, when I faced the devastating loss of my life partner. Traumatized and full of grief, after witnessing his murder in an armed robbery when we were vacationing together, I turned to the arts to heal my shattered spirit.

Art provided me with a tremendous source of solace, a means to express the torrential emotions that flooded through me and a way to find renewed hope and meaning in life.

[9]

Several months into my mourning time, a short story welled out of me. This mythic story contained within it the message that I could not only survive this experience, but also thrive.

The words of the Sorrowkeeper, the wise woman of the story, served to bolster my courage as I traversed the rough terrain of grief and trauma. "Out of your greatest sorrow will come your greatest joy," the Sorrowkeeper tells the young widow in the story. And indeed, the words proved to be true in my own life: I came out of that trauma with greater strength, compassion and the ability to cultivate joy in difficult circumstances.

In the film, *A Song for Africa*, my brother, John Curtin, an award-winning documentary filmmaker, shows poignantly the healing power of music. His film documents the experience of a Ugandan orphan choir as they prepare for and embark on a tour of North America. These children had suffered terrible abuse, loss and trauma. Yet, through their participation in the choir, with the songs and dances that they took joyfully and soulfully to the world, they remade their lives anew, while touching and inspiring audiences with their powerful performances and the strength and resiliency of their spirit.

Another wonderful example is The School of Art and Open Studio of Perquin in El Salvador. Acclaimed artist and human rights activist, Claudia Bernardi, working with local artists, activists and community members, has used art to heal the wounds of civil war. The community has created beautiful murals that both condemn the massacres that took place in nearby El Mozote and simultaneously embrace a powerful vision of peace and reconciliation.

In "Rendering Redemption—Art School Heals Guerilla Town's Wounds" (*New America Media*, August 22, 2006), Josue Rojas paints a vivid picture of what this project has brought to the community:

"Five years and dozens of art projects later, it's an understatement to say that this unlikely school is a hit. People from towns miles away rough the terrain on foot, enthused about the day's art lesson. The classes are jam-packed with farmers and former guerrillas and their children. 'Printmaking classes, drawing classes, jewelry classes, photography classes, video classes—everything that we artists can produce as an offering, the community takes. We have a community of people that believe dearly that art matters. They have

[10]

understood art as a priority because they see what happens with it,' Claudia said."

This inspiring model of art at the service of community and peace-making is now being brought to other areas of El Salvador and to countries such as Guatemala, Colombia and Canada.

You can find out more about this exciting initiative or help support their efforts. Check them out at http://www.wallsofhope.org/.

The positive effects of involvement in the arts have also been recognized for years by healers and therapists all over the world. Indeed, the whole area of expressive arts therapy has developed through this knowledge.

Most of us know the pleasure that we get from engaging in the arts and in seeing art shows, theater, music and dance performances. Studies show that listening to music and singing can have a profound effect on the body and can stimulate the release of endorphins, the happiness hormone.

I noticed this phenomenon when participating in a community choir in Toronto. On cold wintry nights, I had to force myself to get out the door. Just flaking out in front of the TV certainly seemed an easier and more tempting alternative. Often tired from the day and a little grumpy during the first part of the choir practice, I would find it hard to muster any enthusiasm. But then, the music would take over and by the end of the evening, I would feel energized and happy. For the rest of the week, I would go around humming the melodies of some of the tunes we had learned.

Perhaps you've had this sort of experience with art. It takes effort to begin, but just as it is with exercise, once you've started, the satisfaction and joy that comes from the process is profound. Not only is there a rush of endorphins, but the arts also allow you to express and release emotions and find meaning and beauty in life.

Some words from writer, Natalie Goldberg's, *Wild Mind: Living the Writer's Life,* forcefully state the case about what writing means to her and other writers:

"I've never met a writer who wanted to be anything else. They might bitch about something else they're writing on or about their poverty, but they never say they want to quit. They might stop for a few months, but those who have bitten down on the true root do not abandon it and if they do abandon it, they become crazy, drunk or suicidal. Writing is elemental. Once you have tasted its essential life,

[11]

you cannot turn from it without some deep denial and depression. It would be like turning from water. Water is in your blood. You can't go without it." [iv]

Much the same case could be made for the way all artists feel about their art forms.

Although some of us might steer away from becoming artists because of the fear of being unhappy, others may be afraid that being too happy might hamper the creative soul. Even though mental illness and addictions have robbed many artists of their lives and their capacity to work, I have never heard about an artist who was too happy to create. Art making helps us through our suffering and also helps us to celebrate and express our happiness and the beauty we find in the teeming life all around.

Myth #3: The Artist Works Alone in a Garret

The predominant cultural stereotype is of the lone artist struggling by him or herself. Often, this comes along with the belief that to be a true artist, you have to be an outcast or rebel.

Truth: The Artist is Above All a Social Being and at the Center of Society

Instead, many of the arts involve collaboration and teams of creative people working together, especially in the realms of film, theater, music and dance.

For sure, many of us may need time on our own to develop and create our work and some forms of art involve more time alone than others. But in actuality, making art is above all a form of communication. At some point in the process, an audience is involved, even if it's just one other person for whom the artwork is created.

Likewise, although artists have sometimes been rebels and even outcasts in society, in most societies, arts and artists are a vital and crucial part of how a culture defines and sees itself.

Myth #4 – You Have to be Born with a Special Talent to Do Art

Conversely, there is a mystique about being creative. Artists are sometimes thought of as a species apart, as having talents the rest of the population can't access. While artists are not always valued in a monetary way, there nevertheless is a mystique that only certain people can develop as artists. It is often assumed that you have to have artistic genes to be creative.

Truth: Everyone Has Artistic and Creative Abilities That Deserve to be Tapped

Nothing can be further from the truth! Within all of us lies a great well of creative ability. Allowing for and cultivating these capacities in all of us would lead to the greatest flourishing of human culture and society we have ever seen.

Cultivating artistic capacities also enables a person to appreciate even more those who have extraordinary talent, because it is only by being personally involved in the arts that a person can develop the ability to truly appreciate the accomplishments of others. Just as a person who has never participated in sports may not fully appreciate the accomplishments of an Olympic athlete, neither will people who have never taken the time to develop their own artistic skills be able to fully appreciate all the subtleties of a great work of art.

Although I have always loved and appreciated the arts, taking singing lessons and participating in a choir gave me a new appreciation of the skills and abilities needed to become an accomplished singer or musician. I realized how much time, commitment and practice I would need to bring my singing to a higher level. With all my other interests and work, I wasn't prepared to make such a commitment at that time. Nevertheless, I was immensely enriched by the experience, from the fun of learning to sing more songs, to opening up my voice, to developing a greater understanding of music.

Myth #5: To be a Real Artist, You Have To Practice Your Art Full Time

Another belief is that if you are a real artist, you must spend all your time dedicated to your art. And if you have to take another job, it is most likely low paying work such as waiting on tables is something that you plan to quit as soon as you hit it big.

Truth: You Don't Have to Quit Your Day Job to Be a Real Artist

Being an artist has little to do with whether or not you make your living through your art and you don't have to spend all your waking life consumed by it. Indeed, working all the time at your art may hamper your creativity rather than increase it. Doing other things gives you a break, allows your ideas to simmer and brew and may actually assist your artistic development.

Many artists have other jobs, whether it's teaching the arts, employing their skills in the advertising industry, or doing something completely unrelated. Having another job isn't a big deal, although the kind of job you have does matter. If it's a job that requires a full commitment of your time and energy and leaves you exhausted and depleted, then you might consider looking for something that's more compatible.

Sometimes jobs in arts management, although linked to your artistic interests, may be so demanding that they leave little time for you to do your own art work. So don't assume that having a job in the cultural sector is necessarily the best thing for your own art making.

Sometimes doing a job involving physical work can be a good match because it can allow your mind more freedom to roam creatively. I know several artists who've found that having a dog-walking business gives them a solid source of income as well as enough free time to do their art. One client of mine supported herself while going through expressive arts therapy training and then later, her music and songwriting career, simply by walking dogs!

Seasonal work or jobs where you have stints of free time can also allow you a great deal of creative freedom.

One of my clients renovated her basement and made it into a small apartment for visiting ESL students. This allowed her to generate an additional source of income, while leaving her time for her creative projects.

Personally, I find coaching, teaching workshops and doing art a great mix, as it gives me a good deal of flexibility with time and it gives me the ability to undertake artistic projects whenever I want. I've noticed that there are quite a number of coaches who are also artists.

Whether or not you have another job, be sure to allot time for your artwork when you are in a fresh and creative state. Sylvia Plath wrote her novels and poetry before her children woke up. Or perhaps it's late at night when you work best. Either way, make every effort to free up this time for yourself. Otherwise, you'll be swimming upstream.

I used to think that I was only a real artist if I was spending the majority of my working hours devoted to my art or some art-related activity. I once dreamed of the day that I would have the freedom to do nothing but my art.

Now I think differently. When I am in the midst of an artistic project, I can spend almost every waking hour living, thinking and breathing my project. This is particularly true if I am engaged in a theater project and it becomes increasingly so as opening night approaches.

However, if theatre projects come in rapid succession, I become worn out and depleted. I need the balance of my other interests and work and time for my artistic ideas to percolate.

This point was brought home to me after I put a tremendous amount of artistic energy and work into writing, producing and making the masks for my workshop production of "The Sorrowkeeper." After it was done, I had no desire to embark on another big production for quite some time.

That experience, although very fulfilling on an emotional and creative level, also helped to fuel my determination to get out of the *broke-artist syndrome*. I worked on developing other sources of income, including devoting more time to my coaching practice. I didn't give up my art, but certainly the hours I devoted to arts-related work dropped significantly.

I did, however, take a couple of different writing and storytelling classes at Toronto's Gilda's Club with writer and storyteller, Michelle Tocher. I also attended an artists' circle every month, where I would present part of a story or do an improvisational performance piece. I also joined a local choir and began to learn vocal techniques.

In hindsight, that period of very little "professional" work in the arts, when my fields lay fallow, when I let go of my attachment to being a full-time artist, formed the basis for the further freeing of my artistic talents.

The irony is that the less I focused on being a professional artist, the more I was able to artistically express myself with a greater range than I had been able to do previously. And, I began to develop what I called, for lack of a better name, my "artist rants." Much to my surprise, these rants, for which I usually made little or no preparation as they were improvisational in nature, have become very popular

[15]

among my artists friends and other audiences wherever else I perform them.

That being said, some arts require dedicated full-time pursuit, or some artists decide to immerse themselves fully in their art in order to reach the level of mastery they want in their profession. For example, if you want to be a professional ballet dancer, you have to put in many hours each day to keep your body in shape.

It all depends on your own unique form of creativity and where you are in your life. The one-size-fits-all concept of how you schedule your creative development simply doesn't apply.

Myth #6: You Have to Specialize in One Art Form

Even if you are a full-time artist, you may think that you can only excel in one field. There is an underlying message in society that you have to specialize and focus and it is often assumed you can't excel simultaneously at many forms.

Truth: There's No Need to Specialize in One Art Form

My advice, after years of trying to find one singular focus and seeing many other artists becoming frustrated after searching vainly for their "one big passion" is "Don't even try!"

If you are attracted to many forms of creativity, stop fighting it and embrace your many interests. If you love specializing in one art field then "go for it." There really aren't any rules to this game, it's whatever works best for you and your creativity.

I always thought I had to specialize like my parents and many of their artist friends. Both of my parents focused on one field of art. My father, once he learned photography in his early thirties, devoted his professional life to this pursuit. As one of Canada's most accomplished photographers of his time, he found great satisfaction in exploring and deepening his photographic talents. In his later life, he was devoted to documenting Canada's great musicians, combining his love for music (for which he professed no talent whatsoever) with his love for photography.

My mother, a very talented painter, dabbled in acting as a teenager. However, her compelling passion was to paint. She focused her artistic life on painting and continued to work on her colorful still life paintings and landscapes into her late eighties.

[16]

I spent years trying to choose one occupation and one art form, thinking I was somehow missing something if I didn't. I thought that with theater, I had finally found an art form that would encompass all my interests. So for many years, I dived into my passion for theater and in particular, my passion for mask and puppetry.

But that wasn't the way my creativity worked over the long haul and since then, I've been venturing into other art forms, finally accepting the diverse nature of my interests and life.

What I like to do is move from one art form to another. Although theater is the main art form I've practiced over the years, I have no desire to practice it all the time. In a year, I might do one or two theater or visual arts projects that I feel passionate about, write some fiction or non-fiction pieces, participate in an artists' circle where I can experiment with different art forms, lead art or mask workshops and do "artist rants."

Here's an example from 2008, a prolific year of various art making and coaching projects. I wrote and performed in my first one-woman show, did about 20 artist rants, participated in a choir and took part in a singing and sounding performance around a labyrinth. I also led mask and creative life design workshops, worked in my coaching practice, adjudicated a speakers' talent show and took classes and trainings related to my work and varied interests.

Each year is different as my creativity and life shifts in various directions. At the moment, my artistic life is focused on writing, on artist rants and on teaching a few mask and theater workshops. I'm beginning to explore poetry and experiment with some singing techniques as well. And more and more, I've been incorporating my artistic and improvisational skills into my online and offline coaching programs and events, marrying my art with my coaching.

What I actually decide to focus my efforts on is based on a variety of things: an internal feeling of being drawn to a certain type of artistic activity at a certain time, the excitement of the opportunity of being involved in an outside project and the reality of what's going on in other areas of my life at the time. I no longer feel that I have to do my art in any particular way. And that shift in my thinking continues to be tremendously freeing and definitely increases my level of happiness!

I have many artist friends and clients who also thrive on variety. Many of them combine their love of art with other passions such as holistic health and healing, public speaking, coaching, consulting and working for non-profit organizations.

As a coach, one of my big loves is to coach artists and creative entrepreneurs who have many interests on how to create a lifestyle that both incorporates their diverse interests and is financially rewarding and sustainable.

Do you have lots of interests? Do you have a hard time focusing on one art form at a time? Not to worry, you are not flakey or somehow lacking because you love doing a wide variety of art forms and activities. Nor does it mean that you will never succeed.

Yes, at different times, you will need to focus on acquiring a particular skill in one domain, or on a project that involves only some of your artistic or other talents. However, there are many successful artists who divide their time between different art forms and interests. This is not limited to the great artists of the Renaissance, such as Leonardo Da Vinci, but also applies to many contemporary artists who excel in a variety of art forms.

Following are three examples of artists who have created a successful and varied artistic life for themselves.

Barbra Streisand has won Oscars and Golden Globes and many other awards for her singing, acting and directing roles. Less well known is that she has devoted countless hours to her love of design and decorating, which she shared with the world in her book, *My Passion For Design*.

Brilliant Canadian Olympic figure skater, Toller Cranston, not only showed his artistry in his dancing on ice, but he was also an internationally-known painter, illustrator, best-selling author of six books, designer, choreographer, commentator and a star of award-winning television specials and films. His artwork has been exhibited in over 400 gallery shows around the world.

Rock Star and Grammy Winner, Carly Simon, not only topped the charts as a singer and a songwriter, but she has also published whimsical and beautifully illustrated children's books such as, *Midnight Farm*.

Two wonderful books that I constantly recommend to people with many passions are:

1. *The Renaissance Soul: Life Design for People with Too Many Passions to Pick Just One*, by Margaret Lobenstine.

2. *Refuse to Choose! Create the Life and Career of Your Dreams*, by Barbara Sher.

Both these books will allow you to more deeply understand and embrace your diverse nature. These books also provide an abundance of tips and strategies on how to best survive and thrive in a world that often doesn't understand an artist's brilliance.

Your Story

If all the current myths in our culture about creating art aren't enough to discourage you, your early experiences with the creative process may have done the trick. Perhaps a first-grade teacher criticized a painting or a song you had sung. Or maybe someone you loved or respected told you that you basically had no talent. Or someone, out of jealousy, might have made nasty remarks about your creative endeavors.

Or it could be that you are just plain scared of the vulnerability that the artistic process opens up.

In the end, you may feel that being an artist is too hard or too stressful of a life path to be worth it. After all, performing or having your work up in front of people can be extremely stressful and frightening. You risk criticism and even public humiliation if you fail. And even if you succeed beyond your wildest dreams, you will encounter critics who might tear you apart.

Suffice it to say that with these stereotypes and fears, it makes sense that you might be having difficulties following your creative dreams and urges.

Maybe you are concentrating on bread and butter issues and are perhaps even caught up in the lure of consumerism. Although you may be more affluent, you may not feel fulfilled. You may have become divorced from your true self, by giving up this vital source of happiness.

You might be someone who is following your artistic dreams, but who is trapped in a self-fulfilling prophecy of the starving artist myth, finding yourself living from hand to mouth and are simply worried about how to pay next month's rent.

Or you may feel confident in one area of artist expression, but, at the same time, are afraid to try out new things, or to venture out into a new field where you also have talents and creative aspirations.

Perhaps you are stepping back from fully owning your artistic and creative gifts and are afraid to become more visible on the public stage. You may be procrastinating and not following through on publishing and promoting your work, or stashing your paintings under your bed.

Following your artistic soul requires that you gather all your courage and put aside the cultural myths and negative beliefs that can prevent you from stretching your creative wings and flying free.

The first step in this process is to recognize which of these myths you may be living and bring any negative beliefs you have about your artistic self to light. In later chapters, you'll find out how to tame these doubts and fears and move forward with your creative dreams and aspirations.

Questions

1. With which of the stereotypes do you most closely identify?
2. What messages did your family give you about being creative?
3. Did they encourage you, or discourage you from being an artist?
4. What was your experience like at school with respect to the arts?
5. How have these stereotypes and experiences influenced your choices in life?
6. If you had unlimited time, money and resources, what artistic projects would you embark upon?
7. Who are your favorite artists; whom do you aspire to be like?

Action Steps

1. **Set up your "journaling space."**
2. **Find a regular time to journal about these and other questions that come up for you during the process.**
3. **Prioritize the list you made for question 6 above.**
4. **Choose one project, large or small, from your list to focus on for the purposes of this book.**
5. **Decide on and take one small step today toward making that project a reality.**
6. **Pull one book off your shelf that you've been meaning to read that will inspire you as you work towards your goal.**

Chapter 2: Why the Hell Do it Anyway: Finding Your Vision and the Motivation to Keep Going

"The greatest danger for most of us is not that our aim is too high and we miss it, but that it is too low and we reach it."

- Michelangelo

"You have to know what you want. And if it seems to take you off the track, don't hold back, because perhaps that is instinctively where you want to be. And if you hold back and try to be always where you have been before, you will go dry."

- Gertrude Stein

Somewhere in you there is something urging you to explore an art form or undertake a new creative project. It could be something you have done before or something totally unfamiliar, but all you know is that it's nudging at you, coming back again and again.

Will you heed the call? Will you gather up the courage to go on this artistic journey? There are so many unknowns and things you can't control. And in thinking about any new project, no matter how many times you've been through this before, there are the familiar questions that arise: Will you succeed? Are you good enough? Will you have to sacrifice too much? Why is this so important to you? If you make the effort, will anyone care?

So how do you know if it will be worth all the work? You know that the creative process isn't always easy and just that fact alone could cause you to back away from committing to the process. You might even be asking yourself, "Does the world really need one more painting, one more book, one more play, or one more sculpture?"

Be assured that the world can never have too much art and if you put all your care and love and craftsmanship into your creative endeavor, there are sure to be others, maybe many, many others, who will benefit from and appreciate what you have had the courage to share.

This questioning is simply a natural part of any process that involves commitment, especially at the beginning. So here are a few questions to ask yourself that you might not have considered. What would be the cost of ignoring my creativity? What if I just don't do this particular project at this time? How will I feel at the end of my life when I see that I haven't lived up to my creative potential?

This last question is a powerful one. When we remember our lives, what will come to us most vividly, I believe, is the love we expressed and shared, the beautiful creations we lovingly shaped and brought into existence and the contributions we made to the community through our creative and artistic efforts.

So I invite you to value your creativity and give it a sacred space in your life. Each time you turn aside a strong urge to create a work of art or performance, you deprive not only yourself of the joy of creating, but others who would benefit from your gifts.

Remember that each time you embark on a creative project, you embark on a new journey, a journey over uncharted waters, where there are monsters and allies that you'll meet along the way. It doesn't matter whether this is your first creative endeavor, or you've been at this for a while, there will be days when you are so weary that you'll just want to give up.

There will be other days where you'll be filled with incredible energy and joy and feel on top of the world! I encourage you to go forward through whatever internal and external obstacles that show up. Then you will indeed reap the rich treasures of a realized creative life.

Clarifying Your Vision

As with any journey, it's important to map out your intended path and decide on your destination. Of course, that may change as you get into your project, but your intention will help you get started and carry you through when challenges arise. So make a plan for your project and decide where you want to go and what kinds of things you want to explore.

To begin with, here's some questions you might ask yourself:

What type of projects have you been thinking about? What art form would you really love to delve into? Are you interested in combining different art forms within your project? Is this a project that you would like to do on your own, like a series of paintings, or do you want to do a collaborative piece such as putting on a play or directing a film? Do you need to learn any new skills or are you going to use skills you have already developed?

You may have a full-blown image in your mind's eye of exactly what you want to create. Or you may have only a feeling, a few inspiring words that come to mind, or body movements that express this creation you are about to birth. You might have a million different creative ideas that you would love to work on and for you, the difficulty is only in deciding which one to focus on right now.

There are a number of helpful questions you can ask yourself that will help you find clarity. Is there a way you could combine some of the ideas? Is there one idea that is speaking to you right now, that has a particularly strong energy behind it? Are some of the ideas on your list based more on "shoulds" rather than desires? How would this project fit in with the rest of your life?

As an example of my own decision-making process, here is some of what I went through in deciding to write this book.

I had wanted for some time to write a book based on my experiences using the arts and holistic healing techniques to transform grief and trauma. This is something about which I have done a lot of research, writing and thinking. I almost chose to write that book.

However, I was in the midst of shaping a new program designed to help creative people launch and showcase their dream creative projects and my energies were focused around providing the materials for that program

Although I had written a book in my early twenties (*Women In China*), and, as a journalist for several years, had written many articles on current and cultural affairs, I'd never written something that was designed as a personal development tool. Nor had I published a book in electronic form before or tried my hand at self-publishing, so I knew that to write and publish this book, I would need to learn a new set of skills.

I decided that writing a book about fostering the creative process would allow me to try my hand at writing an e-book oriented toward personal growth and it would connect in a meaningful way to my current work and priorities. It would give me the experience I needed and serve as a stepping-stone if, at a later date, I wanted to take on the bigger and more emotionally challenging task of the other book project. At the same time, I would learn about self-publishing.

At the same time, I was also thinking of making some new masks, as well as writing a blog and posting some of my "artist rants." After some consideration, I knew all these projects were important to me and that I would probably do at least some of them later that year. However, my heart was calling me to write this book. I could feel that the energy was there and it made sense in terms of what was going on in other areas of my life.

Questions
1. What art project(s) are you feeling inspired to do right now?
2. Which of those feels most important to you?
3. Why is this project important to you? How do you perceive it will change your life?
4. How will it change the lives of others?
5. If you could convey one message through this particular project, what would it be?
6. If you had a magic wand and you had all the time, money and resources you needed to bring your project to fruition, what would that look like? Describe using as much detail as possible.
7. What exciting and inspiring thing could you do with this project with the least amount of money, time and other resources?
8. Looking at your answers to questions 6 and 7 above, which one excites you the most without overwhelming you? What are you ready to aim for in your life right now? (*Maybe elements of the big vision for the long term and a smaller vision for what you can do in the next few months or year.*)

Action Steps
1. Talk it Over with a Buddy or Coach - If you are having trouble figuring out which idea to follow, you might want to talk it over with a buddy or a coach who has been trained to listen and detect which of your ideas and yearnings have the most energy behind them. It is the energy that lies behind these ideas and yearnings that will provide the fuel for your action and ability to stay the course when challenges arise.
2. Designate a Journal Specifically for This Project - You can use journaling as a tool to help you brainstorm ideas and images you get about your project, as well as write answers to the questions I pose in this book. Having a journal will help you document the process for yourself and serve as a place where you can jot down your feelings and experiences as you proceed on your journey.

3. Create a Vision Board for Your Project - People have used vision boards to express their vision and creative aspirations and to help them manifest their dreams. So why don't you do the same around your artistic dreams and projects?

To create a vision board, the first step is to gather your materials, which include some type of paper, poster board or bristol board, a glue stick, glue, or tape, colored pencils or markers, a variety of magazines or other print material and last, but not least, some scissors. This will serve as the first step to getting your project out into the world. Draw or cut out images from magazines or newspapers and write some words about the essence of what you would like to achieve, how you would like to be appreciated and the kind of audience and venue that would thrill you.

Think big, imagining all the possibilities for what you want to include in your project and convey to your audience and use this expansive feeling to help inspire you to arrange your materials in whatever way you would like on your vision board. Include words or images about how it would impact your life and others. Put down words that express the feelings this project evokes. Feel free to add other materials - fabric, stones, sticks, or found objects. You can also include essential oils or fragrances that evoke something about what you want to create.

Make the vision board as large or as small as you want. Let your intuition guide you. You can always make others, or add to this one later. It can be a source of continued inspiration and will help you to hold your vision throughout your project. Put it somewhere where you can look at it daily.

4. Make Another Board That Reflects Where You Are Right Now – Next, take another board and use images and words to depict where you are today in relation to what you wish to create. What are you starting with, what strengths and talents can take you forward on this journey? Include the materials you already have on hand for your project and the names of people who may serve as resources. The more you use images or symbols to represent your strengths and resources, the more powerful this board will be.

5. Putting it all together - Look at the two boards and record in a journal what you will need to get from where you are currently to being able to manifest your vision. What resources are missing? What actions do you need to take? You don't need to do anything about it yet, this is still all part of the visioning process. You are still just exploring possibilities. Savor this stage. There will be plenty of work ahead. But for the moment, just prepare your mind and your heart for the journey.

Chapter 3: Discover Your Best Working Style: Ways to Get into Action

With our busy lives and many interests, it's often difficult to set aside time for our art making. We have the intention of doing it, but somehow just never manage to get around to it. Although art making thrives on the freedom to explore and to imagine, it is also well served by a structure, framework, or a container.

You may be the kind of artist who is totally self-motivated and finds it easy to set aside time to do your art. You may find that it's not difficult at all to get into a daily routine that helps you to cultivate your creative talents.

My mother was like that with her art. After taking a 20-year break to raise us, her six children, she returned to painting with tremendous energy and determination. Every day, until she was into her eighties, she would go upstairs to her studio and work on her gorgeous still life paintings for three to six hours, seven days a week. She told one reporter, who interviewed her, "I'm a steamroller, I'm happy when I produce."[v]

It wasn't always easy. Many days, when I would go to visit her in her studio, I would see a pained expression on her face, as she was having trouble getting one of the details just right. But she always went up there, no matter what.

Although I had a daily practice of writing artist pages for years, based on Julia Cameron's book, *The Artist's Way*, I must confess to far less consistency in my artist practices than my mother. I am a person who has a lot of difficulty with establishing routines and daily habits, not just in my art, but in everything.

When I first became a mother, I felt guilty because all the parenting books talked about the importance of creating regular routines with one's kids, but that just wasn't my style or temperament. My kid doesn't seem to have suffered too much from this lack on my part and I comfort myself with the knowledge that I have other strengths from which he has benefited.

What really works for me and gets me enthused and in gear, is a project with a deadline, or a classroom structure where I have assignments to complete. Having a specific time frame to complete a project gives me a reason and a structure that helps me focus my energies. I have discovered over the years that this works miracles for my productivity in all my endeavors.

Before I had truly accepted my own temperament and way of doing things, I used to beat myself up about not doing my artwork every day. I wanted to be like my mother and have that discipline and steadiness of a daily art practice. But with time, I have simply learned that I have my own way of working, which is neither good nor bad, it's just my way.

Recently, I came across the work of Kathy Kolbe, which I found fascinating. It talks about how we are all born with an instinctive way of doing things, which we need to recognize and work with. Some, like me, thrive on improvisation and do best working in sprints and doing things at the last minute. Others are the complete opposite and enjoy a more structured approach. Neither way is good nor bad, just different. You can find more information, along with assessments and extensive research she has gathered, at the website, http://www.kolbe.com. I highly recommend you take a look.

Teresa Stratas, a world acclaimed opera singer, told Toronto writer, Ulla Colgrass, "I always work, but I don't do anything regularly. Perhaps I'll get up at three in the morning when I can't sleep and work to the extreme on my music and then perhaps not open a score for the next several days." [vi]

What way do you work best? Do you like doing your art every day at the same time? Or do you like doing it in spurts? Do you work steadily to get a project done, or do you tend to get a great deal done at the last moment?

It's important to know and accept your style and plan accordingly rather than according to the "shoulds" you may have in your head.

Do you also, like me, need an outside deadline or structure to get you going? If that's true for you, make sure that you create a deadline as part of your plan to help inspire you to complete your project.

There are lots of ways to create an outside structure. Which one you choose depends on the type of project you are doing and how far you want to go with it at the time.

One of the best ways I've found to get an outside accountability process going is to make a public commitment to doing a project. I do this with many things, not just my art. I simply tell all my friends that I'm going to do something by a certain date. Often, this is not enough and I will need to follow through on a daily, weekly, or monthly basis with a buddy or coach to report on my progress and

[28]

to clear away any snags that come up.

Sometimes I have applied for an arts grant as a way to get me going on a project, as well as a way to get funding. This, however, can be a double-edged sword. First of all, the grant writing process is often long and involved and I can find myself becoming bogged down in the process. Although it does force me to clarify what I want to do with the project, I can also get carried away and promise to do far more than the grant is possibly worth.

Also, if the grant doesn't come through, it's very easy just to let the project slip. Even when I end up getting the grant, I sometimes wonder if it would have been easier to have just used my other work to support the project rather than go through the whole grant writing process.

What ways can you find to take the first step to committing publicly to your project?

For example, do you want to e-mail all your friends that you have this creative project you are going to do by a certain date? Afterward, you can figure out how and you can always adjust your time frame, but it's a powerful way to get started.

Another good way to get an artistic project off the ground and completed is to join in some type of challenge, which is an inspiring way to get yourself to work quickly and often helps you to blast through any resistance. By looking online, you can find a number of different challenges that are going on in a variety of artistic fields.

For example, there is a National Novel Writing month in the U.S., which has participants from all over the world. In the final stint of this challenge, writers can get together in person for a weekend of writing, with all kinds of prizes offered. It's a lot more fun than struggling on your own and it offers a greater chance that you will complete your work. You can find out more by going to http://www.nanowrimo.org/. They also have a list of similar types of events for songwriting, poetry, play and screen writing.

Finding a group of fellow creative souls in your area to work with can also be a great way to help you stay on track.

Painter, Vanaja Ghose, told me about her experience working with a local art group. "As a visual artist I find that I'll find "other" things to do and procrastinate, so it helps me to be in a structured setting and paint with other artists. We keep each other inspired, critique each other's work and provide helpful suggestions. Just going to one of my art groups and watching another artist's demo inspires me and makes me want to run home and start painting."

I've often run online coaching programs that help people establish a structure for their creative projects to make sure they get them done. Artists from different disciplines work on their individual projects in their home or studio, supported by group mastermind sessions, accountability days and private coaching.

In the private sessions, I am able to help teach participants to define and fine tune their projects and go through any creative blocks they may have. The group accountability days provide a time when everyone works on an aspect of their project and then calls in. The group mastermind sessions allow a place for brainstorming, creative synergy and mutual support that helps take people through the process of artistic creation, promoting their work and getting an audience.

If you don't want to commit publicly, but still want to get going on your project, you might hire a coach who specializes in coaching people through the artistic process. This can be a way to both set up accountability structures, where you report to them on what you are doing and what you plan to do to access your creative artist self.

In my own coaching practice, I find even one or two sessions around an artistic project can often uncover a wealth of material that artists can use to develop their work, which otherwise might have taken a much longer time to coax out on their own. This does require a coach who has a lot of experience in the arts, so that they know what to look for and the questions that will draw the materials out of you.

If you need help around visioning and getting into action around your project, you can find out about my private and group coaching programs through visiting: http://www.katiecurtin.com.

Questions
1. What would you say is your overall temperament and personality when it comes to doing your art? – It's important to take a moment and write about what makes you unique in the way that you approach your artistic work.
2. What is your working style? Do you work best on a strict schedule or do you thrive on variety and change? – It's important to know exactly what inspires you to get into action. The mistake

most people make is to try and follow a model that someone else has created. Take some time to write about and get clear on what type of structure will support you in your efforts to complete your project.

3. What helps you stay inspired and on track? Are you more of a loner or would you rather be part of an artist collective? – When you become conscious of what works best for you then you can take the steps to make that a reality in your life.

4. What keeps you accountable? In the past, what has helped you stay the course and follow through? Some people like to "cave it" and just work without distraction, whereas some people find it very helpful to check in with someone else on a regular basis whether that person is a friend, mentor, or coach.

Action Steps
1. **Decide on a "structure" that will work for you that is customized to meet your personality and your needs.**
2. **Try it out for a week and make adjustments as you see fit.**
3. **If you've determined that having someone to report to will be helpful, find an accountability partner, mentor, or coach to help you stay on track.**

Chapter 4: Planning and Scheduling Your Art Project

Once you have set up an accountability structure for your project that helps you stay on track, whether it is working with a coach, mentor, friend, or just writing in your journal, then you can begin to take the steps toward planning and scheduling the different stages of your project. Granted, everyone works at their own pace and in their own unique way, but the idea is to take the steps and move forward as you become clear about the different aspects of your work. If you are putting on a play or musical performance, you may already have an idea of where and when to book the venue, so you might want to move right away to reserve the space. If you are working on a visual arts project, it might make more sense to do the research and initial phases of your project and wait to book the gallery, or a bigger work space, when you have a better sense of the scope of your project.

Following are a number of actions steps and recommendations that will give you an idea of how you might proceed. Please feel free to use this as a template, which you can customize to meet your own specific needs as they relate to your project or performance.

Actions Steps
1. Choose a completion date.
It's important to be realistic about how you use your time. You know how you work and how long it typically takes you to complete a project, so pick a date that gives you the time you need to comfortably do your best work. If you work well under pressure, choose a date that helps you stay focused but also gives you time to keep balance in your life.

2. Select a date to show your work to others.
Make sure to give yourself plenty of time for all that is needed beyond the creative process. Leave room for all the logistics that go into creating an event.

3. Decide in what venue or context you would like to showcase your work.
Chapter 11, "Finding the Perfect Venue - Thinking Outside The Box," will give you lots of ideas.

4. Create a Flow Chart to Guide Your Course.

A useful way to approach scheduling the overall project is to create a flow chart. Begin by writing your end goal on the right side of the paper and circle it. Then work backward, adding all the action steps you'll need to take to accomplish that goal and circling those as well. Continue to work backward, from the right to the left side of your paper, until you arrive at the action(s) that you can do right away to set the process in motion.

To illustrate my point, let's use a theater production as an example. You know that on opening night, you must have all of these elements in place: actors, production crew, a play, a venue, costumes, props, scenery, lighting, and, last but not least, an audience. For each one, you have to ask yourself what needs to happen for that element to be ready by opening night.

When you look at one element, such as having an audience there on opening night, by working backward, it becomes clear what needs to be done. You need to promote the event. To promote the event, you need people who will distribute the materials, to distribute the materials, you need to create them. To create the materials, you need the information and the money to pay for their production. Using the same line of planning for actors, you need rehearsals to prepare them for the show, for the rehearsals, you need the actors to learn their lines, before that, you need auditions to choose the cast. Continue this process until you come to the first action step that helps you get started with the whole process.

Although some actions can be done in a parallel fashion, others have to go in sequence. A flow chart will help you see which things have to be done and in what sequence. This process will help you keep track and choose the right actions at the right time.

Barbara Sher, in her book, *Wishcraft,* writes:

"Planning has to go backwards from the distant future to tomorrow...from the intimidatingly large to the reassuringly small...from the vision of your goal to its component parts, little things you can do one-by-one."

Barbara suggests that you use two questions as the tools for breaking down the sub goals into the smaller and smaller steps that lead up to them. The first question is, "Can I do this tomorrow?" If the answer is "no," then the next question is, "Okay, what would I have to do first?"[vii]

For each of the sub goals, you need to establish dates by which they should be done in order for the whole project to move forward smoothly. If, when you look at it all, it's overwhelming, look to see if there's anything you can cut, delegate, or break down into smaller steps. If not, change the completion date.

It's important to have your goals to be challenging enough that they get you into action and maintain momentum, but, at the same time, simple enough so as to keep the whole process enjoyable and working with the rest of your life. Build in a lot of flexibility for things that may take more time than you originally thought and for other aspects of your life that might need some extra attention along the way.

When you are doing this type of planning, it's helpful to have your dream board in front of you, as well as the other boards detailing your current resources and strengths. Use any notes you've made about what is needed to get you from the present situation to your dream and incorporate them into whatever action steps you have.

5. Put Your Sub Goal Dates in Your Calendar
Once you've established the dates by which the sub goals need to be accomplished, enter those dates into your calendar. Then consider roughly how much time it will take to complete each task and then schedule designated time in your date book to accomplish each item.

6. Plan According to Your Energy Patterns
Within that overall framework, plan according to what works well for your energy style. If you thrive on a regular schedule and a steady pace, then schedule it that way. If you like working in spurts, schedule some days or weeks that you can devote to your project and other days to focus on another project or aspect of your life.

Also, because there are so many types of work that need to be done outside of the creative process, such as organizing and promotional work, make sure that you take into account what kinds of activities you do best at different times of the day. For example, if your creative energy is high in the morning, use that time, if at all possible, to do your art. Later on in the day, you can make phone calls to arrange promotional details for the project or find out about needed resources and supplies.

When you are planning an extensive art project that covers a long

[34]

time, make sure to include lots of breaks and don't forget to take some time off, even if there seems to be too much to do. With most projects, the last weeks or days before the event will almost inevitably be filled with final details and problem solving for unseen snags. You need to be sufficiently rested and refreshed before the final stretch so you can handle all the final arrangements.

Do your best to pace yourself so that you don't become exhausted. Working on a project can be like running a marathon. You have to be careful not to use up all your reserves in the beginning and to go at a pace that can sustain you over the long haul. That way, during the final days, you can rely on your reserves to help you sprint to the finish line.

7. Schedule Rest Days

Doing art puts big demands on you, wonderful demands, where you really stretch yourself. The truth is that to stay creatively fresh, your body and mind have to rest. If you push yourself too hard, you'll inevitably find yourself making mistakes and making more work for yourself in the long run.

So, right now, go to your planning calendar and schedule in planned days of rest during the project. It's very important to keep those days sacred!

If all this planning makes you feel out of sorts, get a buddy who is systematic in their thinking to help you create the plan. In the following chapter, we'll discuss how to create the time, workspace and money for your creative project.

Chapter 5: Setting Yourself Up For Success: Finding the Time and Space

You may be telling yourself all kinds of stories about why you can't do your art or your dream project. After all, isn't your life already full enough without taking on something new?

Or you may be putting it off, because you think you don't have the right kind of space or materials needed. Or you might be telling yourself you don't have the money or other resources to make your project a reality.

The truth is, you almost always have the opportunity to do your art! Stop believing the stories you are spinning in your mind!

When you make a conscious choice to take on a creative project and then follow it up by even the smallest action step, then the pathway will open up and you'll find the time, space and resources that you need.

First of all, forget all those conditions you put on your art, that you have to give up your current job, that you have to wait until your children are older, that you have to have more money that you have to have the perfect space and situation before you create.

If you want some inspiration from an artist who had every excuse not to do her work just read about how J.K. Rowling found time in the early part of her career. Here's an excerpt from an interview with Heather Riccio for HILARY Magazine, June 21st, 2010:

J.K. Rowling: After I began to write *Philosopher's Stone*, something horrible happened. My mother died. She was only forty-five. Nine months afterwards, I desperately wanted to get away from everything and took a job in Portugal as an English teacher at a language institute. I took my manuscript with me in hopes of working on it while I was there. In my first week in Portugal, I wrote my favorite chapter in *Philosopher's Stone* – The Mirror of Erised. I had hoped that I would've finished with the book by the time I was back from Portugal, but I came back with something better, my daughter, Jessica.

HILARY Magazine: It must have been hard to finish the book now with a small child in your life.

J.K. Rowling: It was hard, but I made it work. Every time Jessica would fall asleep in her pushchair, I'd dash to the nearest café and write as much as I could. I wrote nearly every evening. Then, I had to type everything out myself. Sometimes, I hated the book and all the while I still loved it."

The main point here is that it's better to start right away than not to start at all, even if you are just working five minutes a day.

That being said, here are a few ways to open up your time and also find the space and resources you may need to help you make your dream a reality.

Finding the Time

I recommend that you watch yourself for a day or two. Write down what you do and the time it takes for each activity. Avoid judging or changing anything about the way you go through your day. Simply observe yourself and jot down in detail how you spend your time.

After you have done this, look at your list and ask yourself the following questions. Which of these activities are absolutely necessary for my life balance and happiness? Which activities feel draining and don't contribute to my sense of joy and fulfillment? How can I free myself from these commitments?

Getting Rid of Distractions: How Many Times Do You Have to Check Your Email?

The point here is to see where you might have small enclaves of time that you are using for something that isn't really meaningful for you and that could be used for your art. Do you spend too much time watching TV or checking e-mail? Do hours of your time get sucked up by distractions on the Internet? Are you interrupted constantly so that you have little or no time to focus and get your main tasks done?

One of my coaching clients, a professional writer, came to me feeling overwhelmed. The deadline for a writing project had been suddenly moved up. She had no idea where she could find the time. We carefully went over her schedule to see where she could find some extra uninterrupted time.

It turned out that emails and phone calls had been eating up her time more than she had realized. She decided that for the remainder of the week to only check her e-mail once a day and to only answer the phone outside of her designated writing time.

The amazing thing is that these weren't dramatic changes. It took discipline not to answer the phone or check e-mails when she was writing, however, it allowed her just the right amount of focus to be able to finish the project with ease.

Tim Ferriss in *The 4-Hour Workweek* has some brilliant strategies for cutting down on the type of work that tends to consume our time without giving us what we truly want. He has a variety of excellent tips for eliminating time wasters and advocates the radical approach of only checking your e-mail once a week and then replying to all of them at once.

Depending on your work, this radical approach may or may not be helpful, but even reducing the checking and replying to email once or twice a day, could help to cut down this time waster for many people.

Tim Ferriss, a highly creative renaissance man, who goes for his dreams with imagination and verve, has created many highly lucrative income sources along the way. His book, which is well worth reading, outlines a system for automating and delegating work, as well as creative approaches to business and living.

Batch Your Tasks

Completing any task involves set up time, actually doing the task, then cleaning or tidying up at the end. Some tasks may involve travel time.

That's why batching can be so effective in helping you find more time for your art. This can allow you to cut down on setup, cleanup and travel time, as well as cutting down on the time it takes to transition from one task to another.

For example, deciding to only go food shopping once a week can make a big difference. Putting your errands together can cut down hours of wasted travel time.

Making big batches of food ahead of a major project and freezing them can also reduce the workload. It may require more planning, but in the end, it is well worth your while. In the last days of a project, consider a few takeout meals as a way of getting you through the hump.

Also, sometimes we make our regular food preparation far too complicated. It's great on occasion to make a really delicious and elaborate meal for family and friends, but if you make things simple for daily life, you will free up a lot of time for other ways of expressing your creativity.

I find batching my coaching calls on one or two days a week works well for me. It allows me to get into my coaching mode and have my client files on hand. Then, on other days, I can focus on my other writing or art projects or do other work related to my business or family.

For example, you can batch all of the promotional work related to your project within a few days or half days spread over the months you have scheduled. Batch together the telephone calls you need to make and the trips to pick up the materials you need.

You can batch together the creative part of the process, too. Find out how much time you need to get into high focus on your artwork and then notice how long into the creative process your energy starts to lag and you need either a break or to do something completely different.

I find I work best on a project when I have about three to four hours, or even a day or a whole weekend where I can completely get into a project. However, if I spend too many hours working in a row, I can go into overload. It's important for me to schedule in breaks to go for a walk, take a stretch, or have a meal or snack, about every hour and a half.

How about you? Keep experimenting and notice what works best.

You may find that you work like me, in concentrated dedicated blocks of time, or you may work best in shorter, regularly scheduled time slots each day. Do what works best for you!

Organizing Projects for Easy Transitions
Organize your creative projects so that they are easy to begin and clear away. This can make a surprising difference in whether or not you even get started on a project and can save hours of time.

Gather all the materials you need for a particular project together so that you have easy access and can do something at a moment's notice if you get the urge. Rolling carts or baskets can help you have easy access to your materials. Experiment and see what works best for you.

I worked with a client, who yearned to create some mosaics. Because her materials were scattered all around the house, she couldn't use the pockets of time available to work on these ideas. Setting up and clearing up simply took too long.

The first tasks she needed to do to make sure her mosaic project actually happened involved setting the time aside to buy a rolling cart, rounding up the supplies and tools she needed for the project and finally, organizing them into the drawers of the rolling cart.

This way, even if she only had a short time to work on a mosaic, she was able to roll out the cart to get started and simply roll it back when it was time to put everything away. So instead of spending all that time setting up and clearing away, she had that time to devote to her project.

Find ways to adapt this idea to your art project or activity, however big or small it might be. Perhaps you need only a small box, bag, or basket with your project supplies. Or maybe you need a few rolling carts.

When I'm at the first stage of working on a mask, I need clay, a container of water, a small wooden board, some rags to wipe off my hands, sculpting tools, perhaps a plastic cover to protect my working surface, as well as the images or sketches I might use to inspire myself. I am able to fit all of those things in a medium size basket or box ready to take out and use whenever the muse strikes me.

When first working on this book, I had a black bag with some of my files for reference, a binder with my chapter outlines and ideas and my computer close by. I had a small bookcase close by as well as a box of my favorite art books, which I could use for reference, research, or inspiration.

Time Stretching
Time is very fluid. Often, if you give yourself a very short span of time to do a task, it actually encourages artistic flow and productivity.

Taking a timer and allowing only five to fifteen minutes to write two to three pages without stopping has consistently given people much better results at the beginning of a project, rather than writing slowly and editing every word as you go.

You can do similar things with painting to loosen up. Painting with watercolor or tempera paint in increments of five or ten seconds can yield wonderful, fresh results that can loosen you up and even provide the basis for a more studied painting or project later on.

Taking a piece of clay and making it into a mask or a sculpture in three minutes, might get a more interesting character or form than deliberating about it for hours.

Throw away your assumptions about how long things take and

give yourself short periods where you race against time. It can be lots of fun and surprisingly productive. But also reward yourself with breaks, just like with running, it's important to rest between sprints.

Finding the Space

Now we come to the question of space. Do you think that your art can only be done in just the right environment? Are you waiting for a beautiful light filled studio to do your paintings, sculptures, or performance art? Please don't wait!

I've been there. When I started taking art classes at the university, I decided to join a friend in renting a big art studio, which was quite lovely. I thought that's what type of space I needed to create. The only problem was, I still had many artistic blocks. I did do some painting and drawing in that studio, but I mostly felt even more intimidated and guilty about my art as I was paying a good chunk of my income toward that studio and not doing the work to warrant my investment.

Paradoxically, as I managed to dissolve my artistic blocks and find the art forms in theater that better suited my temperament, I found that I could do art in far less elevated circumstances.

I created over 30 masks and hats for the Canadian Children's Opera Chorus in a tiny room, which was also my bedroom. It was chaotic at times but the work got done.

Another time, I constructed four giant puppets in a small kitchen, which I had to keep clearing so that my family could have it for mealtimes.

Again, none of these were ideal circumstances, but creatively, I got more done than I ever did in my shared big beautiful studio.

So, first of all, start wherever you are. Then if you really can't do your project without a bigger workspace, take the time and find the resources to find the right environment. In Chapter 11 on "Finding the Perfect Venue," you may find some interesting ideas of places that can serve both as a space to create or perform your art and also as a venue to exhibit your final project.

There are many artists who rent studios who would be happy to share expenses. You can work out an arrangement based on how much each of you will use the space, making sure you have the space you need at a substantially lower rate.

Avoid thinking that the outside trappings will give you the inner motivation. This line of thinking can encourage you to spend money needlessly. There are often simple solutions that will serve. Personally, I find that, for most of my projects, I am quite happy working on a table in my living space. It's convenient and I don't have to travel to get there. For projects that have bigger space requirements, I arrange it on a project-by-project basis.

Change Your Environment

Experiment with places and environments to do your art: each space stimulates the imagination in different ways.

I love writing in a café. That's because usually there is just enough noise and people around to make me feel that I'm not alone with the blank page. And, it gets me away from distractions at home. There's no phone or doorbell ringing, or spouse or child to interrupt my thought process.

However, I've stopped going to the local café where my friends hang out if I'm intending to write. Otherwise, being the social animal I am, I can't resist the temptation to chat.

My brother, Joe, a highly innovative violinmaker and writer, has a house and studio on the outskirts of Ann Arbor, Michigan. Even though he has more than enough space in his home, he loves taking time each day to venture out to a local Ann Arbor café to write. He finds that this is just the right environment for his writing and it gives him a break from his house and studio, where he works most of the day.

J.K, Rowling, author of the Harry Potter series, also loves to work in cafés:

"It's no secret that the best place to write, in my opinion, is in a café. You don't have to make your own coffee, you don't have to feel like you're in solitary confinement and if you have writer's block, you can get up and walk to the next café while giving your batteries time to recharge and brain time to think." (HILARY Magazine, June 21st, 2010)

Questions

1. Journal for five minutes about what you tell yourself about not having the time or space to do your art. No censoring, get it all out, however silly it may seem at the time.
2. Now take the ideas from the chapter you've just read and think

about how you can find the space and time to do your project. Again, write without taking the time to edit your answer. (*You may think of further ideas in the days to come, so leave some space to insert those ideas later*)

3. Describe the space that you use to do your art? How is that working for you? What would you like to be different?
4. Is there a way you can organize your art supplies and tools for easy access?
5. In what ways can you batch certain tasks so as to give yourself more creative time?

Action Steps
1. **Follow yourself around for a week and notice what works with regard to time.** Are you able to follow through with your intentions for the day or does something get in your way?
2. **Take careful notes and craft a schedule that batches and streamlines your tasks and is in-line with your personality and time needs.**
3. **Start working to set up your space for your project and to organize your materials and tools for easy access.** If you'll be using an outside venue at any stage of the project ask around and make the necessary contacts to set up and secure a place. (If you're not sure when you'll be using the venue, still make the initial contacts to find out the options for when the time is right.)

Chapter 6: Finding the Money: Getting Creative About Funding Your Arts Projects

You've been finding out how to create more time and space in your life for your art and gaining momentum with your project.

However, you may be wondering how you can afford to follow your bigger artistic dreams? Or maybe you are stalled on a creative project because you simply don't have the funds to purchase the needed materials and supplies.

The idea of generating the money to fund your artistic work can seem overwhelming at times, particularly with the lack of priority in arts funding in even the richest nations of the world.

Arts funding is often the first to get cut in times of economic crisis and even in good times is low on the list of governmental priorities. There are full time jobs in the cultural and arts sector: however, many of these jobs involve arts management and fundraising rather than financing artists to do their art.

Even though you normally can't rely on consistent funding for your arts projects, that doesn't mean you can't do your art. What it does mean is that you have to use your creative skills not just in your art but also in finding the money to make your projects viable.

It's important to first make sure that your beliefs around art and money aren't blocking your creativity in generating more income in your life. Sometimes these beliefs can act as blinders to opportunities that do exist, or they can influence you to spend your money unwisely, leaving you without financial flexibility to follow your creative dreams.

In Chapter 9, "Taming Your Creativity Dragons," I discuss powerful techniques and tools that can help you get through these limiting beliefs, opening you up to avenues that you may not have dreamed possible for your art.

However, outside any mindset issues, there are some important things to consider for whatever creative project you are pursuing.

With each project, it's best to look carefully at your immediate and long-term objectives. Perhaps you are in a phase where you want to freely develop an idea, without the pressure of producing a completed work or going for a large audience.

Those things can wait until a later date, when you feel more confident about your direction and what your idea entails. For this phase, although you may need to make time and cut back on some of your other work, actual costs may be minimal. At this point, it may not make sense to put efforts into getting grants, or trying to fundraise. It's easy to finance it out of pocket.

But, if you are aiming to do a bigger project over a longer time frame, one that will involve a huge commitment of your time, as well as that of other professionals, the renting of venues, the procuring of expensive equipment and materials, along with promotional expenses, then finding ways to raise the capital needed becomes your first priority.

In this scenario, the first phase of the project should focus on raising the money rather than doing the creative work, especially if you are not in a position to hire others to do this work. If you approach this with a sense of fun and artistry, looking to find creative ways to do this, you may enjoy this part of the process.

One important factor in raising money for any project is that you are able to clearly articulate who your audience is and what benefits they will get from your creative project. This holds true whether your artwork uplifts and inspires its audience by its beauty and craftsmanship, or if you're delivering an important social message through your artistic medium.

There are many possibilities to raise money for your artistic projects and endeavors. What follows are some interesting options you may want to explore.

Family and Friends: The people in your life, close friends and family, will often be happy to chip in funds to help you get your project off the ground, or would love to donate their time and services for something you might otherwise need to finance out of a limited budget. Many people are happy to support artists who they love and admire.

Fundraising Projects and Events: From car washes to silent auctions, to selling t-shirts and greeting cards, to hosting galas and other special events, there are hundreds of ways to raise money. Just make sure that the income possibilities merit the time invested. One of the good things about doing fundraising projects is that they also serve a dual function as a way both to raise money and promote and publicize your artistic project.

Ticket or Product Sales: If you are staging a performance or selling artistic products such as paintings or sculptures, some and perhaps most of your income will come from sales of your artwork or tickets to your show. Finding the right price points and choosing the right places to promote or stage your work, all have to enter into your income generation strategy. Making sure you are promoting it to an audience that will be eager to buy, and have the funds to do so, is key. Also, knowing the benefits it brings to the buyers or audience members and doing effective publicity around that is crucial to generating the income for your project.

Online Stores: Online stores, such as Etsy, offer a new option for artists to sell their products, to a worldwide audience. Etsy is a Brooklyn, New York-based global marketplace for arts and crafts that was started in 2005. The sales for 2013 totaled more than 1.35 billion U.S. dollars for the year.

Crowdfunding: Through crowdfunding artists have been able to raise money for their projects in amounts ranging from hundreds of dollars to millions of dollars. This is an exciting new development for artists made possible by the growth of the Internet and online forms of payment.

There are now many sites that help you raise money for your artistic project, whether it be a CD, a film, a book, or other type of project. The better-known sites such as *Indiegogo* or *Kickstarter* can allow you not only to raise money but to build your audience.

Even though these organizations take a percentage of the donations that come, along with a few other conditions, it may be well worth your while to go through these sites rather than simply doing all the fundraising through your own website or web page.

You can use both social media and emails to your distribution list, to ensure that your crowdfunding efforts are successful.

I helped one of my clients, Wendalyn Bartley, an accomplished Canadian composer and sound healer raise $6,000 for a CD project called SOUND DREAMING: Oracle Songs from Ancient Ritual Spaces. She did this through the online fundraising website, Indiegogo. Her friends and supporters donated by either contributing money, or gifts that were used to encourage other people to donate.

To help get the word out, we organized a special "Get It Done

Day," where we invited her supporters to meet every few hours on a teleconference line, to brainstorm promotion tactics and report on what they had accomplished. It involved a great deal of work promoting the campaign, however, at the same time, it helped to grow her audience and got the word out about the CD album.

In an article about crowdfunding, "Kicking the hat around," Alex Gurham writes,

"These campaigns for support aren't solely focused on finances however. Intrinsically built into each effort is the development of an audience, or more appropriately a community. Donators not only become guaranteed product producers, sometimes they are even invited to become actively involved in the work they are supporting. What people are investing in is not a book, movie, or store but the ideas behind them and their development. Inevitably, that development is something each donator becomes personally invested in, not just financially." [viii]

There's an art and science to crowdfunding from how long you stage the campaign to what incentives you offer your supporters. Good planning is essential, as is hard work and keeping at it, even when the going is tough and only a little seems to be coming in.

Arts Grants - Municipal, provincial, or state and national governments all have arts councils or boards that allocate money to arts organizations and projects. Applications can take up a lot of time and effort.

You need to make sure your project dovetails with the guidelines of the particular grant and that you have sufficient credentials and a well-worked out proposal to be successful.

Your credentials as an artist and track record will play an important and even determining role in the success of your grant. Taking great care to prepare your resume and your support materials with photos, audios and videos that powerfully showcase your best work is key.

There are also grants available for people at different stages of professional development, so even artists at the beginning of their careers can find funding if they show potential and have a good proposal.

Your project needs to stand out and be unique; this can be in the form of your artistic expression or it can be that it addresses some important social issue, or through your art representing a cultural

[47]

group that has been under-represented.

For example, over the years, my partner and I have received many grants to do theater projects with students in the Ontario schools.

In these projects, we bring to the stage the myths, legends and history of Mesoamerican culture through theatre, dance, music, mask and puppetry.

This type of proposal is well-received not only because of the wide range of art forms that students get to experience but also because it speaks to the curriculum, which includes the study of ancient civilizations such as that of the Aztecs and the Mayans. My partner not only is a highly experienced actor, director and dancer, but also his knowledge of his native traditions and heritage can convey the culture to students in ways that no textbook can.

Because of the high competition for these grants and the varying tastes and proclivities of juries, you never know whether your proposal will be accepted. I have seen highly accomplished artist friends who have received grants for years, suddenly receive no funding for projects that are of equal or of greater merit.

With hard work and luck, you can get a grant to finance a cherished creative project or to bring your art form into the schools or community. Whether the grant received is large or small, the approval for funding enhances your overall credentials as an artist, helping you as well to get funding from other sources.

Sponsors – Both large companies and small local businesses can often be brought on board to sponsor cultural and artistic projects as a way to promote their products and services in the community. Even if they don't agree to give you money, they often will be happy to contribute in other ways. If you are staging a reception, or selling food and drinks at an event, approaching a local bakery or wine store for donations might substantially cut your costs. A printing company may give you a discount for printing your flyers and promotional materials.

If you are doing a community arts project, or arts heritage project, you may be particularly well positioned to get sponsorship from local businesses and other organizations.

All of these ways of raising funds could merit books on their own and indeed, there are many great books, information products and courses available on these subjects.

A simple search on Google or Amazon can yield a multitude of resources.

But before you race out and buy more on this subject, think deeply about what you want to accomplish with your creative projects and which ways of raising money most closely dovetail with your overall objectives. Which way would raise the most money with the least effort? Which would be the most fun to do?

The idea of creating a team of art patrons to support your project will be discussed in Chapter 8. This team of art patrons can be key in helping you brainstorm and carrying out fundraising for your project. Team members can also be invaluable sources for helping cut the costs of the project, through connections for reduced rental fees for space and equipment, obtaining donations of materials, etc.

Questions
1. What would you say is your overall relationship with money?
2. Are you making money with your art?
3. If not, is that something you would like to change? In what way?
4. Which of the suggestions in this chapter regarding raising of money could be useful for your current art project?

Action Steps
1. **Make a list of all the ways you make money and create an income/expense chart.** Although it's not always the case, as an artist, it can be easy to lose track of the practical details of how much money you are making and where it all goes at the end of the month. I recommend that you devote some time weekly or monthly to keep track of the flow of money in and out of your life.

2. **For your arts project, create a budget of your projected expenses and income.**

3. **Begin investigating funding sources for your project, based on your budget needs.**

Chapter 7: Exploring the Terrain: Finding Inspiration and Ideas

The best way to have a good idea is to have lots of ideas.
- Linus Pauling

To live a creative life, we must lose our fear of being wrong.
- Joseph Chilton Pearce

As with any trip, you've made your plans, found the time and place to go and now you've arrived and are ready to explore the new terrain ahead of you.

This can be a really fun, liberating part of the artistic journey, where you collect ideas and explore the different possibilities before you. Like a trip to a foreign country, it's great to open your mind up to all the new stimuli that's coming your way, to new perspectives and ways of looking at things.

Capturing Your Ideas

I recommend that you always keep a little notebook or recording device with you so you can capture your ideas right when they come to you. However you keep track, the important thing is that you have something that is easily accessible any time you have a new inspiration. You may think you'll remember the idea later on, but, sadly, that is usually not the case.

Above all, listen to your inner voice and the whispers of potential. Get everything that floats into your brain down on paper or taped, whether it's writing down thoughts, sketching images, or recording a fragment of a song. It doesn't matter if the drawings aren't beautiful, the words aren't perfectly crafted, or the melody is off. All that matters is that you capture the images, sounds and words as soon as they come to you in the moment.

This is not the time to use your powers of judgment for what works or doesn't work. In this first stage of the journey the important thing is to give yourself the freedom to try things out before you settle on a final form. So exile your perfectionism and be prepared to do lots of what you may consider bad art.

Getting everything out, good and bad, gets you through the terror of the blank page or the blank canvas and allows your creative right brain to do its work. Later, you can pan through and find the golden nuggets, throwing out what doesn't work and refining and polishing the rest.

If you are having a hard time getting down to your creative work, try micro-movements, which are very tiny actions toward your goal. It might be getting your painting supplies and brushes ready and telling yourself you just have to do one brush stroke for the day. More than likely, one brush stroke will lead to another and it will be hard to tear yourself away from the canvas. This is a great strategy for procrastination in general.

Finding Inspiration

With all the emphasis on originality, sometimes artists will be hesitant to look at the work of others for fear of being influenced by what they see. I am of the opposite mind. I think the more work of other artists you can expose yourself to, the better.

It doesn't mean that you copy them. Just look at what they are doing and notice what appeals to you. Be aware of what you don't like. This will help inform you about what you do want to create. Additionally, when you have a special project in mind, you will be more perceptive than normal, more naturally curious about what others are doing. You may find an idea that you can adapt and use for your work, whether it has to do with the choice of materials, the treatment of a theme, or the way the materials are being handled.

Perhaps a painting by Georgia O'Keefe might inspire you to zero in and magnify a part of a flower. Or you could adapt that idea by magnifying a part of the human body such as someone's lips and make it fill the whole canvas. Or you might like the colors and hues of a particular painting and use them in a weaving you are doing or a glaze for a ceramic piece.

Libraries are wonderful places to find inspiration, particularly in the kids' sections, where the books have lots of illustrations. Books on nature can also give you an endless source of ideas. Just looking at all the amazing underwater animals and plants can stimulate wonderful ideas for sculptures.

On the subject of nature, a great way to give yourself a break is to take a stroll through the woods or through a park. Looking and listening can provide you with ideas for many artistic projects.

Other techniques you might find helpful in the beginning phases

[51]

of work are storyboarding or making a small model of something you want to build.

Storyboarding, first developed by Walt Disney, is used in the film industry to pre-visualize the scenes of a movie by showing a layout of events as it will be seen through the lens of a camera.

Others have adapted it for different media, such as the design phase of web sites and other interactive projects. A number of puppetry artists I know use a storyboard when designing their shows and I found it very useful when I was working on writing and staging my play, "The Sorrowkeeper."

Because I was adapting my play from a short story I had written earlier, the storyboard allowed me to translate the story for the stage and visualize the scenes. Because we were integrating ritual, dance, theatre, live music, masks and puppets and having many of the actors play multiple roles, storyboarding helped me see how the different elements of the production would weave together and to visualize the rhythm of the play.

You can also add words to your storyboard to convey the atmosphere, the sounds, or the music you want. All this helps to further stimulate your imagination and helps you conceive your ideas more fully.

Create Your Project in Miniature
Similarly, you can create a "maquette" for a set or a room design or a small version of a larger sculpture you want to make. This allows you to try out on a miniature scale what you are envisioning. It allows you to experiment and see what works before you take the time, effort and materials to build the full size version.

I've emphasized some techniques in the previous chapters that will get you working fast as a way to bypass your internal critic and to help produce lots of ideas and material for your project. However, it's also good for your creative muscles to take periods where you slow down and revel in doing something very small and detailed.

For example, take extra loving care to mix the perfect color you want for your painting or to mold that particular part of a feature in a sculpture that fascinates you. Take time to revel in feeling the materials and instruments you are using.

Do a movement incredibly slowly to find all its potential. Or make a contour drawing by very slowly tracing the edges of the objects, people and scenery you see, without looking at the page while you are doing it. Or take one little stone and take your time to draw its every detail.

Going at varying speeds, or changing pace, going from small to big and back again, all contribute to heightening one's creativity by providing a means for the mind to think, see and feel in different ways and make new connections. After all, the basis of creativity is the ability to see with fresh eyes and combine familiar things in new and different forms.

Another way to do this is to switch from one art form to another and back. If you are sculpting, go and write about or sing your sculpture. If you are singing, talk or draw your song. Dance the picture you have just sketched, then go back to the original art form and bring what you have discovered. It lightens up the process and you have a lot of fun as well. And that's a good thing!

In Chapter 13, "Keeping Inspired - 11 Ways to Fire up Your Creativity," I will present suggestions to keep you from becoming stuck and more tips for how to further develop you artistic work.

Questions
1. What is the overall vision of your project?
2. If you were done with your project and you were standing in front of a group of possible patrons, what would you be showing them on this day?
3. Where do you derive the most inspiration?
4. Who do you look up to as an artist? Who are your artistic heroes and heroines and why?
5. What works best for you in terms of capturing your inspirations and ideas?
6. Where do you tend to find the most inspiration?

Actions Steps
1. **Make a flow chart or map of your project** - Write down as much as you can about anything that relates to your project, so that you have a sense of the big picture as well as the end goal as you can imagine it right now. Include as much detail as you possibly can.

2. **Make sure you have a reliable way to capture your ideas in the moment** - If you already have something, great, but if you don't, take some time to create a system that works for you and your temperament. The most important thing is that whichever way you keep track it should be easy to locate things when you most need them.

3. **Make a list of all the places you like to go when you are blocked** – often times, when we hit a rough spot in regard to our creativity, we are the least creative about where we might need to go to get unstuck. So, having a list that you can access might help you to change your perspective and give you some fresh ideas about where you want to go with your project.

Chapter 8: Finding Support: How to Develop Your Dream Team of Art Patrons

If you want to do an artistic project that you take out into the world, it requires a lot of your creative energies and it helps tremendously to have a support team who will help get your project out into the public eye. It's also helpful to have a supportive group of people behind the scenes to whom you are holding yourself accountable, because you won't want to let them down and having them will motivate you to push yourself forward, even when you are discouraged or are feeling stuck in the process.

I'm not talking about people who are involved in the creative part of the project, such as the other members of the cast and crew in a theatre production or the other members of a singing group. In fact, it is better if your dream team is made up of people who aren't burdened by any of the creative demands, but can give you support in other ways: helping spread the word, providing technical advice, or just being there on the opening day for moral support.

Being a support person doesn't have to require a huge commitment. In some cases, it may only require a day or two of their time. Believe it or not, some people are delighted to be asked to be a patron of the arts and are willing to help you in whatever way is most helpful to you.

One of my friends, who had many books to her credit, planned to attend an out of town writers' festival. Friends of hers, who had a beautiful house in front of the property used by the festival, offered her the use of their courtyard for a book reading and also as a space for a book display.

Although my friend wished to take advantage of this opportunity, she felt less than enthusiastic about spending the day mostly by herself promoting her books. Her friends who offered her the space were busy with other parts of the festival and weren't going to be available to be with her.

I suggested that her other friends and fans, who were coming to the festival, might be delighted to come and help to promote her book. She took me up on this idea and asked a number of her friends, including me, to come along to help her out.

The day began rather inauspiciously with pouring rain, but luckily, within a few hours, the rain had stopped and the sun came shining through. People began to flock to her table at the festival and we all helped to inform the curious people about her books, as well as her writing and storytelling workshops.

Later, just before the event was over, we went out and announced the book reading and ushered people into the courtyard. One of her friends, a radio talk show host, gave a rousing introduction, which she followed with a spirited and dramatic reading of sections from her book.

Afterward, the audience had a chance to participate and ask questions and she brought out champagne to celebrate the occasion. Not only did she sell books that day, but those of us who helped out had a grand time!

So just remember, you don't always have to go it alone in promoting your work, nor do you always have to pay for help. You have friends and family who would enjoy getting together and supporting your work. There are plenty of people who are looking for opportunities to volunteer their services for good causes and why shouldn't you consider yourself an excellent investment of time?

Set up a Board of Art Patrons

For more ongoing support, you can set up your own Board of Art Patrons. You could meet with them once a month over a three to six month period, depending on the nature of your project. These people can help you to brainstorm ideas, find resources, help with publicity, raise funds and find venues for showcasing your work.

A good way to ask people to be on your support team is to create and send a short e-mail that talks about the vision for your project and inviting them to become members of your Board. You could perhaps spice up your request with the promise of front row seats or some other special little opportunity or gift you can offer them.

Recruit People with a Wide Range of Talents, Expertise and Experience

In forming a board, begin by contacting via email or a phone call, more people than you actually need, as there's sure to be a few who although they would love to support you, have a lot going on in their own lives and won't be able to commit the time. Also, contact people with a range of different experiences and backgrounds; include people who have practical talents and abilities you might not have.

Then when you have a committed group of about 5-12 people, call the first meeting. Be sure you are prepared with a description of the project that includes your main objectives and overall mission statement. Also, to help people really understand what you are looking for, you need to have clear ideas of the areas in which you need help. And if there's something you're stuck on, brainstorm it with them: people love to find solutions to other people's problems and will be happy to help you with your challenges.

Your once a month meeting can be a potluck that serves both a business and a social function. That way, members will have the opportunity to get to know each other and make new friends, as well as having a chance to work with you to support your project.

There are so many ways people can help out.

They may be willing to e-mail or telephone their friends about an event you are staging, or they may be interested in ushering or selling tickets or serving food at your opening show. They may be able to get materials you need for the project at a discounted rate or have ideas about how you can get them for free. Or they may be able to connect you with people who have expertise in something you need done. Some members may be willing to approach local businesses to get sponsorship for your event.

Keep in mind that what you find burdensome, another person may love to do.

It's important to get others involved in ways that use their capacities and gifts, making sure they are doing activities they enjoy. They will appreciate the opportunity to participate as well as be invaluable help for you.

Having a group of loyal supporters will make a big difference in your ability to get out into the world with your project. And what's more, it will foster friendships and community. And we all need more community!

Above all, be sure to show your appreciation for their efforts and give them recognition in any program or other written material that you produce for your project.

[57]

Questions

1. Have you ever asked anyone to support your artistic pursuits?

2. If so, who have you asked and how was that for you?

3. If you could assemble your "Dream Team" of artist patrons, "really think outside of the box," "no holds barred," who would you include?

Actions Steps

1. **Create a wish list for your project -** It's important to make a very specific list, exactly what you need just for this project. It can be easy to start thinking about all the things you need as an artist in general, but being specific can help you to focus and makes it much easier for others to support you in a way that will truly make a difference in your efforts.

2. **Create another list of people you could imagine supporting you either emotionally, monetarily, or as a volunteer -** Go through all your address lists and you will be amazed at the number of people you can write down as people who would do something to help you along the way.

3. **Go through your list and decide whom you would feel comfortable contacting -** Divide your list up into the categories that make sense for your project: volunteers, friends to call when you need an emotional boost, creative people who are good with ideas and those who would possibly be interested in funding the project.

4. **Make a realistic commitment as to how many people you will contact each week and stick to it -** You may want to set up an accountability partner to help you stay on track with your promise to yourself. Just make sure that whatever you decide to do, that it feels good to you, that way you won't end up sabotaging your efforts. For instance, if you've set a goal that wasn't realistic, adjust your plan to fit what works best for you.

Chapter 9: Taming Your Creativity Dragons

Creativity is our true nature; blocks are an unnatural thwarting of a process at once as normal and as miraculous as the blossoming of a flower at the end of a slender green stem.

- Julia Cameron

To live a creative life, we must lose our fear of being wrong.

- Joseph Chilton Pearce

Just as you will meet creativity allies on the journey to create your artistic dreams, you'll also meet up with creativity dragons that can scare you off your path. They are often voices inside you that express internal fears based on difficult past experiences rather than your present life situation. But they can also come from outside of you in the form of negative comments from friends, family, or even strangers who criticize your artistic work and aspirations.

It's important to remember that these creativity dragons can come up at any point along your journey and that they need to be addressed so they don't end up running the show.

A common fear is that what you are doing is not "good enough."

This is a fear I hear constantly from clients and it's something I've confronted time after time in myself. In writing this book, I've noticed this constant harping voice in my head saying things like, "this is trite," or "how is this any different than all the other books out there," or, the mother of them all, "who do you think you are to write this book," and on and on. A woman in one of my online writing groups, called her critic, her inner librarian, describing her as a severe and disapproving character who told her to "be sensible" and asked her in a nasty tone, "Do you call yourself a writer?" This character was more concerned with rules and regulations than creativity and certainly was out to kill all the fun, the fun her inner child delighted in when she was writing freely. This fear of not being good enough often manifests itself in either procrastination or perfectionism, either in not doing your art, or spending endless time trying to perfect a small part of it.

In her book, *Loving What Is*, Byron Katie says these wise words, "If I had a prayer, it would be this: "God spare me from the desire for love, for approval or appreciation.""

This is true in all aspects of our life and particularly true with our art. We can become absolutely paralyzed in our artistic pursuits by the fear that our work may not be appreciated, that we may fail to impress or that people may not like what we've done and think badly of us.

Fear of visibility has been a huge factor among many of my clients. Some of these fears originate from childhood experiences, whereas others are born out of family traumas going back generations. Centuries of sexism, racial discrimination, war and genocide have profoundly impacted our psyches, causing deep fears of being seen. I can't count how many times I've worked with women, who have past life memories of being killed or burnt at the stake as a witch.

Within the last two months alone, I've worked with three different clients who found themselves paralyzed in their creative projects because of fears linked to memories of the witch hunts. One woman told me that a part of her believed that if she went out into the world with her message, she would be killed and that she had deep cellular beliefs related to the witch hunts.

In my coaching practice, I have seen time and time again, how, when such traumas and fears are released, using different energy techniques described later in this chapter, clients no longer have to work against enormous inner resistance and because of that inner shift, have much greater ease and success in both doing their creative work and in promoting their work in the world.

Also, I have found it doesn't matter if you believe in past lives or not, if such memories come up in a session and are cleared, the resulting relief from anxiety and fear can be huge.

There's a very interesting paradox that exists in art making. We have to be conscious that we are creating our artwork for an audience; that it is a form of communication, a way of creating beauty and magic and of giving other people pleasure. However, we cannot be bound by the dictates of trying to please those people when we are doing our art.

We should listen to our inner voice, to the inner truths that art creation reveals. We have to have our sensitivity and intuition tuned in to the message that is contained within the medium and the story we are creating. During the creative process, if we turn our attention to what people may think, or how they respond, we deprive ourselves of the true nature of art and what our soul is trying to express.

[60]

Art is an examination, a noticing and extracting from life of its lessons and essence and then conveying that through the molding and shaping of our artistic medium. It is the expression by our bodies or our voices of our individual and collective experience of joy and sorrow and of the mysteries of the universe. It a cry of rage against injustice, it is a celebration of beauty, it is an examination of our own and others' values.

It is not through pandering to our ego's need for acceptance that we find such truth, because in doing so, we turn away from the call that shapes our art and toward the voices in our head that dictate and create those boxes in which our creativity cannot thrive.

All the technique in the world used to dazzle the eyes and ears of others is of little avail when we are not tuned into the soul of our art and the deep message it wants to convey. Of course, when technique is married with the full expression of the soul, it is a marvelous thing, but never let your concern for impressing others let you forget the true source of your art.

The truth is that part of the job of being an artist is to be a warrior for your own soul project, the artwork you know the world needs, even if its message will not be understood by all and may meet with opposition or even rejection.

These qualities of courage and tenacity that the artist must have often don't receive full acknowledgment, but they are the protectors of your creativity. Take a moment and think about how you can be a warrior for your creativity. Summon up the inner courage that lives inside of you along with the deep knowledge of artistic truth that needs to be aired.

You might assume that because I came from a family of artists, it would be easier for me to come into my own with respect to my creativity. And indeed, I'm truly grateful for being surrounded by art and artists as I grew up.

However, like so many children of talented artists, the bar was set high. My parents didn't encourage me as a child to develop my artistic gifts. I grew up thinking that I had to be an artistic "genius" on the level of Picasso, or at least "world class" to merit becoming an artist.

When I first thought about quitting my work in the railways to follow my artistic dreams, I imagined members of my family whispering behind my back, "It's a pity she's decided to become an artist, she doesn't really have the talent." These thoughts effectively stopped me in my tracks for many years.

I steeled myself against my inner critic, who kept saying, "You are not really creative," "Why bother," and "You will never succeed at this," and, step-by-step, went toward my dreams.

At that time, I knew little about how to tame my "Creativity Dragons" of fear, uncertainty and doubt, or how to rid myself of old patterns from the past.

Years of walking the artist's path, working with my own fears and those of my clients, I have learned many powerful techniques and ways to make the going easier.

Your beliefs profoundly shape your life experience in ways you can barely imagine. When you change a belief, you can change your entire experience, which then helps you to stop repeating the same old patterns of self-sabotage. But the question that comes up is always, how can you do this?

One way to create new thought patterns is to replace negative thinking and beliefs with positive ones. Start simply by reframing your beliefs about your artistic life. Instead of mindlessly replaying the old tapes in your head, press pause and listen to what you tell yourself. Every time you hear a negative statement in your head about your art or your creativity, question it and turn it around, so that you gradually chip away at your negative beliefs and replace them with positive ones.

Plant new seeds so that you can live fully in the joy and manifestation that art making can bring rather than surrounded by the litany of negative feelings and lack of possibility.

That being said, sometimes we need to clear away the garbage of old beliefs through more than just focusing on the positive. We need to come face to face with our dragons.

Fortunately, a lot of techniques developed by the human potential movement allow us to quickly and powerfully dissolve old beliefs that seem to be controlling our lives. They can help us with performance anxiety and with the terror and paralysis that makes creation almost impossible.

How to Tame Your Creativity Dragons

One technique I learned during my coach's training is outlined in the book, *Taming your Gremlin: A Surprisingly Simple Method for Getting Out of Your Own Way,* by Rick Carson. It asks us to personify all our negative beliefs into a gremlin figure.

Do this right now around all the negative stuff you think about your art and creativity. You can make it a gremlin, or a monster or a dragon. Imagine and draw a creature that says all these nasty things to you and is full of this negative and pessimistic talk.

This creativity dragon might be saying things like, "Forget it, you're not creative," "You just don't have the drive to do it," "It's not worth the effort," "Why not just enjoy life and take it easy, art is just too much of a bother," "You won't have time to do the other things you need to do, like put food on the table," "You will be abandoning your family," "Nobody is going to like it," "You don't have the skills." On and on your dragon will go, sucking you down into its dark despairing vortex.

What you have to remember is that, buried within the negative messages, there is some truth in what your dragon says. So don't just cavalierly ignore him or her and forge ahead. In fact, believe it or not, your dragon's voice comes from the part of you that's trying to protect you from pain. So give it credit, listen with curiosity to what it says and see how you can use the information in a positive way to make the whole process more joyful and sustainable. For example, how are you going to organize your project so that you do have time for your family and friends and aren't hopelessly stressed out? Maybe the dragon has a good point about enjoying life and taking it easy, or that you need to give your family more attention.

Maybe you've been neglecting your other needs. How can you make the process of the project as enjoyable as possible? How can you plan some special events with family during and after the project? Are there any ways you can involve them in the project, so it builds family relationships rather than taking time away from developing and strengthening those relationships?

Then, after having recognized that part of you that your creativity dragon is trying to protect from pain, gently and firmly tell your dragon to go back to his or her cave, while you move on with your project.

Other Techniques to Dissolve Artistic Blocks

Sometimes, however, your dragons are too big and powerful to yield to these techniques and you may need to use other magic. Sometimes, you need to go deep into past losses, traumas and family issues.

Neuro Linguistic Programming (NLP), the Emotional Freedom Technique (EFT), the Z-Point for Peace Process, Body Talk, Access Consciousness and the Healing Codes are among the methods I have used to free myself and my clients, of old beliefs and traumas.

Also, the techniques of Byron Katie, outlined in her book, *Loving What Is,* are simple to learn and very powerful, in unblocking negative beliefs and thought patterns that get in the way of doing your creative work.

There's a multitude of other methods that work to release blocked energy. Or if you already have a favorite modality that works for you, use it.

There are now many excellent videos on YouTube, showing you how to use these different energy modalities. Often, big changes can come from simply tapping on meridian points, while bringing up words, images and feelings related to the issue. It's difficult to believe how such simple methods can bring such powerful changes. But they do. Try it for yourself and see. If your creative blocks are strong, you would do well to explore these techniques and work with a coach or therapist who has training in the energy therapies.

I've developed both private and group coaching programs to help artists and creative entrepreneurs to get through these internal blocks and negative patterns. This includes my Matrix Transformation Club and my popular Money Matrix program. I've found that mindset is often the number one obstacle to people getting their artistic projects out in the world. You can find out more at my website at http://www.katiecurtin.com.

Questions

1. Do you have any creativity monsters or dragons in the form of negative self-talk?
2. If so, what is it they say to you? What conditions in your creative process trigger their responses?
3. Do you have people in your life who criticize your artistic talents and aspirations?

4. Have you ever been criticized in public for your artistic contribution?
5. When you feel disempowered either by internal or external messages, what helps you to feel empowered and re-inspired to keep going with your work?
6. Do you have any special therapies or techniques that have been particularly helpful for you?
7. Are there any people in your life you can turn to when those negative messages become overwhelming?

Action Steps

1. **Keep a journal of your ups and downs in regard to your creativity and motivation to keep going -** You might be able to see a pattern and then devise a structure or practice that will help you move more quickly through those times.

2. **Learn one of the techniques and use it when needed -** Make some choices about learning a technique or including a practice that will help you to feel more grounded and confident in your choice to follow your heart.

3. **As an antidote for when you become discouraged, make sure to spend time away from your art just enjoying life** – It's easy to become unbalanced in how you spend your time, especially when there is a deadline.

   Sometimes, getting away and getting a new perspective on life is the best thing you can do to get out of a negative feeling.

Chapter 10: Staying Engaged - 11 Ways to Fire Up Your Creativity

As you work on your project, there may be times when you feel blocked or stuck. The following tips can help you move forward with your project and get you unstuck when you are not sure what to do next. Some of the ideas will work for all art forms and others, although applicable, may need to be adapted for your particular form of artistic expression.

This chapter is designed for you to use as a tool whenever you feel the muse has left you. So whenever you need a boost, come back to this chapter and scan through the ideas. One of them may be exactly what you need to push through to the next level of your project.

Tip #1: Use the Subconscious
Give directives to your subconscious to bring you ideas and solutions for your project. If you are blocked in any part of the process, ask your subconscious before you go to sleep to work on the problem you are trying to solve while you are sleeping. Make sure you have your notebook beside your bed in the morning so you can capture any dreams or thoughts you have upon arising.

Tip #2: Take a Walk or Run
Actually, the idea is to engage in any form of physical exercise that gets your endorphins going. These endorphins will keep you positive and will heighten your creativity.

I find that walking or running, particularly by myself, helps clear my head and makes way for all kinds of ideas regarding the project I am working on. I think there's something about the rhythmic motion, along with the time on one's own to think that is helpful.

A similar process happens when I am alone on a train. I get all sorts of ideas as I watch the landscape go by. There's something about the movement of the train that is conducive as well. I can't back that up with a study, it's simply my own personal experience.

Notice for yourself what works for you to clear your mind and come up with new inspirations.

Tip #3: Make a list of fun places to do your art and go there

You may be able to do different aspects of your project in other places rather than where you usually work. A new environment often helps stimulate your imagination and opens up different ideas and ways you might approach your project.

Tip #4: Use Templates, But Give Them a New Twist

People do this a lot in business to save time and to get away from the terror of the blank page. They copy a structure for writing something like a sales letter, an article, or a letter to a customer and then adapt it to fill their needs.

In the artistic realm, Shakespeare did this by adapting many stories, folktales, legends and historical events and made them his own. In turn, others have used his themes and plots to create films, plays and musicals. "West Side Story" and "Rosencrantz and Guildenstern are Dead" are two examples.

You can also combine something old with something new. For example, put an old story in a contemporary setting. This is done all the time in Hollywood.

Tip #5: Watch a Disney Movie

Disney films are brilliant examples of using a template and mixing elements to create something new. For example, when I was first writing this chapter, my son, Tonatiuh, was watching the film, *Hercules*. I was feeling a little blocked in my writing process, so I decided to watch the movie with him. After just a few minutes, I was ready to return to my writing with a fresh perspective.

The film is obviously based on a lot of research about the ancient Greeks, their gods, their myths, their art forms and their daily lives, which is incorporated into the visuals of the film as well as the script.

They took an old story, *Hercules* and by putting it into cartoon form, made it highly entertaining for children. They also mixed in elements of modern culture. For example, they have a "Greek Chorus," an element used in the ancient plays, but this chorus looks and sounds like it just stepped out of a popular song and dance video. You may or may not appreciate Disney, but he was a creative genius and it is well worth looking at how his formula works and use it to help you in your own creative process.

Tip #6: Look for Any Object and Make an Association

What happened with the movie was that when I was stuck, I looked out at my environment. It could literally have been anything that had sparked my imagination, it just happened to be a Disney movie that was playing. But in actuality, I could have looked at any nearby object and asked myself how it could inform my process.

Let's just do this again

There's a chair in front of me—I look for a relationship between that particular chair and the theme of creativity. Here are some ideas that come to me in the moment.

- The idea that you use a chair to rest leads to the importance of resting during the creative process.

- The chair has a beautiful orange-checkered cushion on it. That leads me to the association of a checkers game and from there to chess. I remember a production for which I created masks. The director, Ida Carnavali, incorporated the idea of a chess game into the staging of Faust.

- The chair is also very nicely crafted, which leads me to think about craftsmanship and the taking of time to really refine and craft whatever you are working on.

Tip #7: Use Mind Maps

This is a great method to stimulate creativity and brainstorm ideas in any area of your life.

You begin by writing down your topic in the middle of a piece of paper and circling it. Then you draw lines branching out to all of the ideas that are sparked by the original topic. In turn, these ideas will lead you to branch out into other ideas and so on. If you Google "mind maps," you will find the many programs that allow you to do this on your computer.

If you use a piece of paper, you can add colors and symbols that help stimulate your imagination even further. I highly recommend at some point that you get one of Tony Buzan's books on this subject. He pioneered this system and his book, *The Ultimate Book of Mind Maps*, provides wonderful examples of how to get started.

Tip #8: Enter the Story from a New Angle

My friend Michelle Tocher, who is a brilliant storyteller, writer and purveyor of the magic of the fairy world, has developed an extraordinary system for how to delve into and experience the power of myths and fairy tales. You pick any character in a story or myth and then choose different moments to enter the story and imagine what you are seeing and hearing and feeling from the point of view of that character or object.

It's been fascinating to participate in her workshops and see all the different stories and angles that can come out of one fairy tale, told by different people from different vantage points.

To see some examples of this method, you can visit Michelle's website at http://www.michelletocher.com. Her site also features an interview with me on my exploration of the Cinderella story. I have used this method to develop a number of ideas, including the ideas that led to the writing of the script for "The Sorrowkeeper."

Artists I know, from many different artistic disciplines, have had their own creative practice enriched immeasurably by participating in her workshops.

Tip #9: Find a Coach Who Can Get You through the Sticky Points

Sometimes you just need someone with experience in the creative process to coach you through a place where you feel stuck. I've often booked a session with Michelle Tocher, when I feel creatively challenged and she helps me walk through my imagination to find the way out of that stuck place.

Similarly, when I feel bogged down in some kind of negative belief and can't seem to get through to the other side using techniques on my own, I will work with another coach to find the roots or the belief system to release their hold.

Like all coaches, I know that you can't always do for yourself what you can do for others, so I never hesitate to call on my colleagues when I become stuck. Similarly, if I find a client needs an expertise that I may not have, I am happy to refer them on.

Tip #10: Look at Your Artwork from a Different Perspective

Turn everything on its head, turn it sideways, backwards: look at it from as many angles as you can. If you are doing a painting, turn it upside down. If you are doing a dance, do an opposite kind of movement. Try singing a popular song like you would an aria or vice versa. Even as creative people, it's interesting how you can get used to the way you do things and forget to change things up a bit by changing your perspective.

Tip #11: Look at Art from Different Cultures
Experience different cultures. Look at the ways they do their art and experiment. It can give you great ideas and help you to take off your cultural blinders.

Chapter 11: Finding the Perfect Venue - Thinking Outside the Box

For some of you reading this book, creating and enjoying your own art on a personal level is all you're after. But I'm assuming that most of you are interested in sharing your creations with a larger audience. Art is a form of communication and a powerful form of shared soul experience.

The nature of your project and the level of confidence you feel in your particular endeavor will help you to choose your venue. For those of you who aspire to showing your work, after all the time and effort you've put into your project, one thing is certain, you probably don't want your manuscript or drawing to remain a secret, collecting dust on the shelf, or for your theatre or dance piece to be performed for a painfully small audience.

In your original vision, you may have had an idea of how the final presentation would go. Now is the perfect time to revisit your original intentions and goals. It is important to weigh each goal carefully as you decide upon your venue because it will make a big difference in the overall outcome. So as you consider what venue you would like to use, ask yourself the following questions:

How many people would you like to be there to see and appreciate your work? Why did you choose that number? What number stretches you out of your comfort zone and yet is realistic at this stage of the game? If you are planning a really big event, what resources do you need to ensure that it all takes place as you envision? Will your need to promote the event get in the way of making creative time available for your project? Are you thinking too small, or are you biting off more than you can chew?

Now this might also be a good time to consult with a coach or trusted friend for a second opinion. Or you might want to bring these questions to your board of artist patrons to find out what they think about the possibilities and how they might help.

The venue you choose makes a big difference in how much work is involved in the project, the amount of financial and other resources you must mobilize and the profit you can ultimately make. Think carefully about your objectives. How much money do you need to earn to make the project viable and what is actually needed for the creative purpose of the project to be realized?

[71]

To help you get started, following are a few suggestions for places to show your work.

1. Your Home

This can work really well for visual art projects that aren't too big: small to medium size paintings, sculptures, jewelry, etc., fit into this category. My sister, Philippa, has done this brilliantly; over the years, she has often hosted shows in her home of her custom designed jewelry, masks and paintings.

Sometimes, she organizes a Christmas showcase where she exhibits lovely clay Christmas ornaments she has designed, as well as her other work. She is also a great cook and provides guests with a range of absolutely mouth-watering sweet treats. She spends a number of days before the event doing all the cooking, but on the day of the showcase, so that she has time to talk with guests about her artwork, she hires a local person to come in to help serve the guests.

She always has a full house, and, quite frankly, once you've been there, you are happy to be invited again. Not only do you get a chance to see and buy her artistic wares, but you also get to nibble on fantastic food and mingle with a really fun group of guests.

2. A Friend or Patron's House

If you don't have a house or are not particularly skilled in the cooking department, this is a perfect opportunity to call upon your trusty dream team for help. One of them may be delighted to host your event and there may be others who would love to volunteer to help with the cooking, set up and clean up.

3. Musical or Artistic "Happening"

A couple I know, who owned a beautiful mansion, hosted an annual Christmas Fair, which included fine art and crafts as well as holistic products. As well as being a delight to attend, the event served as a lovely and festive occasion for artists to showcase their work.

For many years, Toronto writer and journalist, Ulla Colgrass, together with her husband, renowned composer, Michael Colgrass, hosted Sunday brunches and invited musicians they knew to play for the guests. This wonderful gathering helped to foster community and connections, while providing an intimate venue for musicians to share their passion for music.

Note: Just be aware that showcasing your work at home venues won't necessarily provide a huge margin of profit and in some cases, may provide none at all. You may save on venue costs, but you also have to factor in the time involved, as well as all the other expenses related to entertaining guests in your home.

Also, if you decide to organize such an event, or series of events, make sure to be realistic about the time and effort involved and how it works into the rest of your life. That being said, it's a wonderful way to develop an appreciative group of fans and foster a warm relationship with people who may either buy your work or refer you to others.

4. An Empty Warehouse

An empty warehouse can be a great venue that you may even be able to get for free from a local business owner who has access to an empty space. The unusual nature of these spaces also opens up interesting possibilities if you are staging a performance.

For a few years, I shared a warehouse space in a mall that a local puppetry artist and writer managed to get rent-free. I used the space to hold mask workshops, to create my own artwork and to stage a play, for which I served as the assistant director. It was a huge space that neither of us would normally have been able to afford, so it saved each of us a lot of money. Later, the owner had the opportunity to rent it out as a commercial space and regretfully, we had to find other options for our artistic work.

5. Local Ruins

These are delicious places for performance work, because they lend so much to the imagination and there are usually not a lot of costs involved. Whenever I go past a building that is half in ruins, my imagination starts to fly about how a performance could give those ruins new life. However, depending on what you are planning, the expenses may mount up if you have to outfit the venue yourself and rent seating, lighting, sound equipment, etc.

6. Parks, Islands, Recreational Areas, Local Farms

For outdoor performances and installations, there are an enormous number of options. Peter Schumann's Bread and Puppet Theatre

[73]

provides a marvelous example of creative use of space. For many years, they staged an annual pageant at their home base, a farm in Vermont, performing spectacular shows with giant puppets. Over time, they developed a loyal following of tens of thousands of people who attended these yearly gatherings.

For their shows, they employed a team of professional theatre artists, who enlisted the help of hundreds of volunteers to build the puppets, masks and props and to stage the performances. They served stone-oven baked bread to die for and hearty soups to the participants. People even camped in the fields of the farm.

It was an experience that I will remember for the rest of my life. I especially enjoyed seeing the shows and meeting all the creative people who came to those events. I attended twice and both times, I found myself entranced by the evocative, archetypal beauty of the puppets as well as the performances.

Enormously stimulated by the experience, each time, I would return home with a storehouse of creative ideas. I loved perusing their barn museum chock-full of masks and puppets from past productions and I still look at my photos from those festivals for sources of inspiration.

The Bread and Puppet Theatre eventually stopped doing the Summer Pageants at the farm and turned their attention to other projects. The rich traditions they established in the use of giant puppetry and pageantry in outdoor spaces continues to influence popular theatre and puppetry groups throughout North America and beyond. Their use of giant puppets at anti-war rallies and other radical events has been noticed and copied by other artists and activists around the world. I've personally been involved in many demonstrations in Canada, where giant puppets have served to draw public attention to the protests, adding color and drama to the event.

7. Boats

A writer friend of mine, Michelle Tocher, carried out an unusual and creative launch of her book, *The May Queen*, on a large sailing boat. Women wearing dramatic hats and costumes took tickets, while friends and fans filled both decks. We all had a wonderful time listening to the readings and chatting with other artistic souls.

At the end of the event, each of us received a free copy of *The May Queen* and one of the colored ribbons with quotes from the book, which had been flying festively in the wind on the top deck. The eccentric, splashy central character of the novel, May, would have adored such an event. That's what creative showcasing is all about to me, sharing our gifts with friends and community and finding fresh and innovative ways to do just that.

8. Ponds, Lakes, Beaches
The Vietnamese have a tradition of staging puppet performances in water. I have seen some variations of this also done in Canada. Outdoor theatre groups such as Toronto's Shadowland and Jumblies Theatre have done some wonderful productions on beaches. As with all outdoor productions, if you go down this road, you will need to make provisions for weather as well as for lighting, sound and seating.

9. Cafés and Storefronts
Cafés and local stores are often happy to exhibit the work of local artists. There is usually a built in audience already coming to the café, which makes it a perfect venue to showcase your work.

Before you decide to exhibit at a café, consider the type of people who go there. Are they likely to be people who would respond to and buy your work? If you do secure a showing, make sure that you have a way to gather contact information of those interested in further showings. Brainstorm ways to encourage more drop-in traffic.

One of my favorite coffee houses in Toronto, Ellington's Café, has become a hub for local artists and community members. As well as superbly brewed Fair Trade coffee, the Café sells music CDs, features local artist's work on the walls and has frequent performances by a range of excellent local musicians. Winston, the owner, is a musician himself, and, from time to time, performs with his reggae band. They feature open mic nights, where you can try out a new song, read your poetry, or tell a story. The local Hillcrest Village Choir has used the space for both practices and performances and it provides artists of all kinds a place to chat and hang out. In addition, this coffee house gave the neighborhood a new and revived sense of community.

10. Parades and Carnivals
Often, there will be parades and carnivals where you may have an

opportunity to perform, create artwork, or show creations you have already made. Even though a lot of these festivals may not pay a lot, this allows you to become better known, get your work out and adds to your portfolio, which will bolster your chances of success with grant applications.

In one of my first puppetry commissions, I constructed a giant puppet of Bob Marley for a Toronto Caribana parade contingent. I made the puppet in a common room in an apartment building at Jane and Finch. I had a great time working there and hanging out with the locals. I was able to get photos of the project for my portfolio and used these photos in grant applications for Artist in the Schools residencies and for other arts projects.

11. Libraries, Schools, City Halls, Parks and Other Public Spaces

Because people are already there, these spaces can serve as great venues for different artistic ventures. Also, because these places frequently host festivals and shows, they often have performance facilities. Colleges and universities often have excellent theater and arts facilities that you may be able to use, even if you are not enrolled as a student.

12. Art Galleries, Arts Buildings and Studios

These can be places not only for exhibiting visual art, but also can be used for other performances as well. Often, a smaller art gallery that is looking to increase traffic might be happy to let you use their space for an evening performance. Or there could even be a local artist or artists' group that would rent you their studio for your event at a lower rate.

My sister, Caroline, a talented sculptor, helped to spearhead and organize an art exhibit at the Mont Orford Arts Centre in Quebec, which showcased art works from our entire family of eight, including photographs, paintings, sculptures, masks and giant puppets. My brother, Joe, exhibited some of his violins and gave a lecture on his techniques and discoveries in creating world-class violins. I directed a collaborative performance piece with my sister, Mary. She read her poetry, performing with masks I had created.

My father's photographs of accomplished Canadian musicians and my brother's lecture and exhibit about violins, tied in with a local

[76]

festival of music that was going on at the time. And in addition, the whole project fulfilled the arts center's mandate, which was to combine the visual arts with music.

Combining the different art forms, along with the performance and lecture, made it more of an event, which was well received by the public. In addition, the angle of a family of artists doing a collective exhibition intrigued people and even attracted coverage by the local press.

This idea of a multi-media event can be taken up and adapted by any group or collective of artists from different disciplines. It provides for the effective cross promotion of each other's work and makes an event that's more intriguing for a local gallery or arts center to host. Having a theme that unites the exhibit along with performance elements helps to unify the event and provides interesting angles for promotion.

13. Artist Residency Facilities

These are great venues for getting your work done and can give you a chance not only to have quiet time to do your art, but also the opportunity to create friendships and share ideas with other artists. There are also sometimes opportunities to showcase your work in certain facilities provided. Res Artis is an association of over 490 centers, organizations and individuals in over 70 countries providing artist residency opportunities. You can get more information from their website at http://www.resartis.org/en/.

14. Festivals

Festivals are being held year round and can be an excellent way to showcase your work to a larger audience. One huge advantage of showing your work or doing a performance at a festival is that the festival organizers typically do the work to bring people into the show. That's the way we have done many of the productions of The Fifth Sun Theatre Company, of which my husband and I are co-artistic directors. We did our first production together at Toronto's Tarrragon Theatre Spring Festival. An interesting thing happened though. The burning of copal incense in a ceremony at the beginning of the play actually set off the theater's fire alarm. But despite our not-so-stellar first performance, it later led to an invitation for our company to perform at Toronto's Harbourfront Centre.

15. Theaters

The cost of many theater venues has gone up tremendously, as I discovered when I was looking for space for my workshop production of "The Sorrowkeeper." In major cities like Toronto, most theater venues often cost thousands of dollars for even a short run. The great advantage is that if the venue is well known, you get into their official lineup and they already have an audience of theatergoers looking for plays to attend. The other great advantage is that they take care of all the logistics such as box office and ticket orders, securing ushers and setting up and monitoring refreshment and concessions areas.

After doing the workshop production of "The Sorrowkeeper" in a venue that had a stage but provided no box office or other services, I certainly learned a lesson about how much effort is required to take care of these functions in an effective way.

Theaters often host festivals where they make their space available for free to participating groups. This is a great opportunity to showcase your work in a theater without incurring huge venue expenses.

16. Showcases organized by Arts Councils

In Ontario, as well as in other provinces in Canada, you can pay a fee for you or your company to participate in annual showcases where producers come to check out talent. These are great events where you can make contacts with other performers, producers and directors and learn more about the different theaters and venues that are interested in bringing in performing artists.

Questions
1. Describe your ideal venue? Include all the senses: what does it look like; what type of acoustics would you like; what type of food do you want and so on.
2. Considering a list of places you already know about, what is your dream location?
3. If you couldn't have that space what would be your second choice?

Action Steps

1. Make a list of the places that would be possible venues for your project.

2. Schedule a check on venue availability and take the necessary steps to secure the venue for your project.

Chapter 12: Powerful Promotion - How to Get Your Project a Large and Appreciative Audience

Even if you are being showcased in a place that has a built in audience, it's important to do some of the promotion yourself. Here is where your Board of Art Patrons can be an invaluable resource in getting the word out and perhaps finding you free promotional opportunities. In this chapter, you will find a medley of ways you can promote your work.

Advertising

In general, I wouldn't advise spending money on paid advertising. There are more effective and cost-friendly means to promote your work. If you do choose to run ads, you need to do them over a period of time to have impact. Also, very carefully choose where you place your advertising, so that it reaches an audience who is likely to be interested in buying your work or attending a performance.

Press Release to the Media

By all means, do your best to contact local media about your work once you begin showing publicly. You can usually find a local person or a person on the Internet who has media experience and can write the copy for your promotional material. They may have a list of the media outlets in your area and beyond.

If you decide to write it yourself, here are some basic guidelines to follow.

You need a hook, something that will entice the local media to pick up your event. Ask yourself a few questions: What makes your event special and newsworthy? Is it taking place in an unusual venue? Does it address an important issue that would concern a specific audience? Does it deal with a topic that is currently in the news? Or does it link up with a local festival or with a particular season or holiday celebration? Think about the press release, not from your point of view, but from that of a journalist and what they might be looking for. What makes you and your project unique and worth talking about?

Also, remember to keep the information short and pithy and make sure you include the who, what, when and how of the event you are promoting. A good press release only needs to be a few paragraphs and no longer than one page. The more professional you are in the way you present the information, the more likely any promoter in the media will pay attention and want to write about or announce your event.

Look on TV and the radio to see what programs might feature the type of work you are doing. Local newspapers are often looking for stories and are happy to feature local artists in their publication. The trick, as with anything these days, is to actually be able to get through to people. Remember their c-mail boxes are probably even more overflowing than yours. You may also want to send some hard copy press releases to well-chosen media sources you particularly want to target.

After sending out a press release, follow up with calls to the editors and representatives of local media. Remember to check in with your friends and your Board of Art Patrons about the contacts they have in the media and how you might get in touch with them. You may be surprised at how many media sources you can get through to in this way.

In my early twenties, I worked as a journalist for Montreal's Town of Mount Royal Weekly Post. I was always on the lookout for interesting local arts events and was delighted to feature an artist from the area when I had the opportunity. Many weeks, I had to stretch things to find a newsworthy event and I was grateful when an artist would stroll in or write to us with a press release or item for the events column.

When I think back on the job, I realize how few artists actually approached us to get in the newspaper. How were we to know of their existence unless we already had some personal contact with them? Even if they were famous, we might not necessarily be aware that they lived in the newspaper's catchment area.

When preparing the workshop production of "The Sorrowkeeper," the overwhelming amount of creative work we had to do to prepare for the performance left little time to approach the press in a thorough manner. Yet, surprisingly, with a press release, a few well-placed phone calls and use of personal contacts from the cast and production crew, we managed to get a lot of radio coverage. We were particularly successful in getting on a number of campus radio shows as well.

We were featured on Toronto's Aboriginal Voice's Radio with a panel of speakers about the impact of grief and loss in First Nations communities. Our media coordinator, Patricia Visser, who was Metis and active in the native community, arranged the interview. A number of the cast and crew members, including J.J., who played the Sorrowkeeper, were First Nations members and had experienced multiple losses of loved ones themselves.

Grief and loss is a huge issue for everyone. But for the First Nations community, this is even more so, with the history of genocide and racism against their people and its legacy of despair, poverty and addictions. So there was a natural link between the play, the target audience of the radio and the challenges the audience faced.

One of our biggest opportunities came when J.J. and I were asked to do an interview for a program on CBC Radio, Canada's national radio station. After the interview, my phone rang all day long with people who were calling to tell us how much they loved what we had said on the radio show and were wanting to buy tickets for the performance.

Events Columns in Local Newspapers

Although you may not always get featured in all the newspapers and media you might like, usually you can get a free listing in their events columns. Make a list of these and their deadlines for publication and compose a few sentences that give the essential details of your event. There are also usually a number of free online community calendars where you can list your event.

Make Sure Your Friends and Workmates Know

All too often, when doing a production or show of my work, I have left off contacting my friends and acquaintances until rather late in the process. I have spent more time getting the word out to people I don't know.

Yet, most of us, even some well-known in their artistic field, garner a significant part of their audience from their own social circles. I certainly noticed this not just at the shows I've participated in, but also at the openings I've attended for other artists. Some exceptions include the shows in the big theater and music venues and the large community art shows and festivals.

In big cities like Toronto, where so much is going on culturally, you would do well to focus your promotional efforts on getting the news out first to the community of people you already know. Cultivate and appreciate your local friends and fans and keep them posted on your arts events and productions well ahead of time. If asked, they, in turn, will be happy to spread the word.

Growing Your List by Using the Internet

Just like any business, creating a list of people who are interested and likely to come out to your events can be one of your greatest allies in creating long term success. There are many ways you can grow your list by using online media.

Also, people on your Board Of Art Patrons or your friends may have substantial lists that they would be willing to contact about a specific event.

Having a regular newsletter that talks about your artistic projects and contains some articles about the art-making process can be an extremely effective way of building a relationship with your audience and fans. You can have an item in the newsletter that encourages them to pass it on to their friends. You may want to use a reliable Internet company such as AWeber to automate the process of sending out e-mails and news to your contact list.

Having a web site or blog site, where people can see examples of your work and where there is an opt-in box that allows people to sign up and hear about your events and products, is a key element in promoting your work these days.

Setting up and maintaining a website doesn't have to be a costly affair. Using WordPress, you can create both an attractive and functional website for free and update it yourself easily. Unless you are tech savvy, I advise you to get someone to do the initial setup and design for you. You can get a site done for a few hundred dollars and it's well worth the investment.

Weebly is an even easier alternative to set-up and use than WordPress and has all functions you need to set up an attractive and functional site.

Social Media

There are a huge number of possibilities to grow your audience and contact list through the intelligent and focused use of social media strategies. I say focused use, because it is very easy to waste huge amounts of time online if you are not clear about your focus and objectives.

Artists are using Facebook, MySpace, YouTube, Twitter, LinkedIn, Pinterest, Google + and many other social media sites to promote their artistic offerings. It took me a few years before I began to enjoy social media, because I'm not a techie. However, now, I enjoy YouTube and Pinterest. My favorite social media site, however, is Facebook. It's a great way to reconnect with artists and friends whom I've met over the years and keep in touch with what they are up to, as well as to get to know other creatives. I also use it as a platform to promote my classes and other events.

It is also easy, once you know a few basic things about these sites, to set up an account, create pages that feature you and your work and any events you are hosting by posting comments, photos and videos. It costs you nothing to set up a Facebook account and it allows you to promote your work to the fans you already have and provides an easy way to extend your reach.

If you are able to do a short video clip of your work and post it on YouTube, it can be one of the fastest and most effective ways of getting your work out to the world. If it's good and you start by sending the link to friends and they like it and send it to their friends, in no time, hundreds or even thousands or more will know about your work.

Promotional Material
As well as press releases you send and the information you post on the web, it is important to have off-line material that you can give out to people. For smaller events, it can be as simple as a flyer you design on your computer and then photocopy and post in strategic spots around town.

For bigger events, unless you are a graphic designer, you would do well to hire one to create the poster, flyers and other promotional material. This is a place where you can easily spend a lot of money, so be clear about what you really need and budget accordingly. Check out the graphic designers on fiverr, for prices you can't beat at https://www.fiverr.com.

If you are looking to make a business card to promote your art and you want to keep down your initial costs, a relatively inexpensive online option is Vista Print, http://www.vistaprint.com.

Many artists are now making effective use of color postcards, which form an attractive and relatively inexpensive form of promotion. You can usually make a thousand postcards for just over two hundred dollars. You can mail these out to your list of friends and patrons and post or leave the cards in community centers, cafes, stores, galleries and anywhere else you think your target audience hangs out. You can also use these and any posters and flyers you print to recognize your main sponsors.

Organize Distribution Teams

Make sure you have a strategy to get promotional materials distributed and posted once you produce them. It's more effective and more fun to organize teams to do this. If you just leave it up to individuals to take your promotional materials, you have no guarantee that they will actually get, around to distributing what you have given them. I would hate to imagine how many posters and postcards lie around collecting dust and then finally get chucked, just because people were too busy or preoccupied to remember to do as they had promised. Teamwork makes sure it gets done. This is one more way your Board of Art Patrons can help you. You can also hire someone, usually at a reasonable rate, to put up posters in your area, saving you time and headaches.

Action Plan for Promotion

At an early stage in the project, you will want to look at your overall objectives and choose what promotional strategies you are going to employ. You want to balance your need for creative time with your need to promote your work once you get it done. Make sure you consult and work with others around this process, whether it is your Board of Art Patrons, your buddies, or a coach.

Also know that the business and marketing side of an art project is very important. If you have no experience in this area, it will take you time, training and patience. Start small with things that come easily to you and then build on them. Above all, get others to help you during this crucial part of the journey! The following is a list, which outlines the steps you can take to promote your event.

Action List for the Promotion of Your Project

Here's a basic list of actions you may want to take to promote your artistic work and projects. One thing you can do is write down all the steps that apply to your project and create a timeline of when it would be best to take care of each item on your list.

1. Compile a list of the names of all friends, family, colleagues and work mates who might be interested in coming to your events. Enter them into a database or create a group mailing list in your computer address book or CRM (Client Management System).

2. Check in with friends who have mailing lists and contacts. Ask if they would be willing to do mailings for your event or share your work with potential supporters.

3. Send out e-mail or a newsletter describing your new project and showcase dates.

4. At various points during the project, send updates to your list on your progress.

5. In your e-mail updates and promotional materials, mention and give appreciation for the help you are receiving from friends and your Board of Art Patrons, along with any sponsors you are able to bring on board. This all helps build momentum.

6. Collect images and write all information necessary for the design of promotional materials (postcards, posters, flyers, etc.)

7. Meet and collaborate with a graphic designer for design of promotional materials. Go to http://www.elance.com and http://www.fiverr.com to access a host of graphic designers available on the Internet at a range of prices.

8. Finalize your promotional material with designer. Proofread! Proofread! Proofread!

9. Deliver and pickup promotional material from printers.

10. Organize teams to put up posters and distribute postcards and flyers.

11. Ask everyone you know if they have any contacts with press and media.

12. Collect a list of names, phone numbers, addresses and e-mails of all local media, as well as any national media you may want to target.

13. Write a press release and send it out to your media list.

14. Follow up press release with calls to media you wish to target or where you have personal leads.

15. Prepare and go to any media interviews you procure.

16. Promote your event on any website or social media site you have set up.

17. Arrange for design and printing of the program for your event. Use this to recognize all participants and sponsors, as well as a promotional piece for you and your work. Be sure to include contact information, so people can get hold of you in the future and any website address you have.

18. Have a signup list at your event to collect names of people for your e-mail and newsletter lists.

19. Afterward, send out an e-mail to your list, thanking all those who attended and helped make the event a success. Highlight the wonderful things that happened through the creating and showcasing of your project and the efforts of your Board of Art Patrons.

Chapter 13: You Did It! - Completions, Celebrations and Next Steps

"Creativity is allowing yourself to make mistakes. Art is knowing which ones to keep."

Scott Adams

"When you get into a tight place and everything goes against you, till it seems as though you could not hang on a minute longer, never give up then, for that is just the place and time that the tide will turn."

Harriet Beecher Stowe

"The more you praise and celebrate your life, the more there is in life to celebrate."

Oprah Winfrey

After gathering the research and working with your ideas for your project, after all the time you've put into experimenting and crafting your work, now is the time to evaluate what you want to use and what you want to let go of.

Although earlier, we talked about how important it is to put aside your inner judge and let things flow, in this last stage of the project, it's important to call upon your powers of discernment to help you refine, polish and edit your work.

The Importance of Feedback
At this point, it's extremely helpful to have someone else help you, someone you know and trust and who has values and a vision that is in sync with your own. It should be someone who understands and has experience in your particular art form.

In theater, for example, if you are one of the performers, the director is often the one who gives you feedback. At this stage, some directors will even call upon other directors to come in and take a look. The main point is to find someone who has a certain distance from the project and can be more objective to come in and give you their opinion on how things are going.

This is also the time when you may be spending a lot of energy refining your work in order to get all of the details just right. If you are an actor, musician, or dancer, a lot of time will be spent rehearsing to get the role or piece inside your bones. If you are a visual artist, this time may be spent on one small area of the page or canvas. You may be focusing on the places where you have difficulty, or you may be focusing on the overall feeling of what you want to convey to your audience.

The important thing to remember is that this stage takes time, patience and lots of work and it may seem that you will never be ready to show your work or be ready for opening night.

I know for myself, a week or so before the due date of a theater project or a big writing assignment, I often have no idea how I am ever going to get it finished to my satisfaction.

In my mind, I'm thinking about how I've already put in so much energy and am wondering if I can sustain this level of intensity through the last sprint. My "creativity dragon" may try to take over and drag me down into his pit of doom and gloom. He may even succeed for a short while.

However, as an artist, I have now been through this enough times that I have a deep inner knowing that I am capable of rallying my energy and successfully moving through to completion.

So be aware that not long before the finish line, although things may appear to be impossible, to keep your faith alive and keep plugging away. In the final day or two, rally all your energy for the final sprint to the finish line.

Opening Night and Beyond

You are now ready to take your work to an audience. You are both excited and nervous about how it's going to go. This is natural. It's said that if an actor or a performer has no fluttery feeling at all, the performance may be flat. The adrenaline rush of the big night can be used to your advantage by channeling all that excitement into your performance.

If you are a visual artist or director, there is nothing more you can do but relax and take in the show. For all involved, there needs to be a letting go. Your artistic work is now in the hands of the audience to appreciate and evaluate. Whatever their response, you can be proud of all the ups and downs you have gone through, as well as all the inner and outer obstacles you have overcome to bring your artistic work to fruition.

[89]

As I write this, I'm thinking about the time I participated in a marathon to raise funds for the opponents of the military regime in El Salvador during their civil war. I remember the final sprint and how I arrived half-limping, but totally exhilarated to cross the finish line. My time was certainly far from that of the champions and I arrived toward the end of the pack, but here's the thing...I had reached my goal of completing the race and had used all my strength, capacity and endurance to get there. And for that, I was proud.

You can feel the same way about your creative project, even if the results don't always match your biggest visions. As an artist, finishing one project allows you to go on to others, in a constant state of learning and polishing your skills. You will notice areas for future growth, where you can do better next time.

Avoid letting your inner critic and creativity dragons take away the pleasure of crossing the finish line by harping on the little things you could have done better. Focus on celebrating what you have done and how much you have learned through the process.

Action Steps:

1. Celebrate!
Be proud of what you have done. Celebrate not only the accomplishments and the final outcome, but also the courage it took to make it to the finish line. Celebrate the whole journey and process you went through to complete your project. Don't forget to celebrate the small steps you took along the way! Celebrate the deepened friendships that may have developed during this project and for the light and color you brought to the world by sharing your gifts and talents. Give gratitude to all those who have helped on your journey and for all the learning the journey provided for you.

2. Reward and Rest
In the days after opening night, or when a show has finished, take a break. Make sure you really take time to rest and recuperate. Treat yourself to something special and perhaps indulge in a little luxury, such as a day at a spa or a weekend away. You deserve it.

The biggest mistakes people often make is not to fully acknowledge their accomplishments or give themselves the rest they need after a sustained effort to reach an important goal. They rush on to their next goal without savoring the sweet fruits of the harvest.

As well, avoid being alarmed if you feel a little down after your project ends. I often have a day or two after a big project is finished of feeling blue and at loose ends. I miss the creative rush that I have been experiencing and often, the close contact with the people I had been working with for so long. Experience has taught me that these feelings are temporary and soon, I am again enthusiastically involved in my daily life.

3. Wrap Up and Begin Again

After you've taken a rest, it's important to take some time to do the wrap up work around the project and tie up any loose ends. You may have reports to do if you have received a government grant for the project. You may have bills to pay and accounting work to complete. You will have thank you notes to write to those who have helped. You may have a party to plan and organize.

This is some of the least glamorous work of an artistic project, but it needs to be done so that you have closure and so that you can free your mind for whatever is next. Make sure to schedule the time to take care of all the details and then to put an accountability structure in place to make sure everything gets done. Don't forget that you can enlist your volunteers or Board of Art Patrons to help you with this aspect of the process as well!

During this wrapping up process, keep your artistic process alive by giving yourself some time for your creative side. Even doing something very small can help to keep your creative fires kindled.

As you move on to whatever is next, this could be the perfect time to take an art class or any class that interests you. Maybe you just want to take the time to just think about, take notes and sketch about a future project. Or maybe you want to set up a monthly gathering with artist friends to brainstorm and experiment with new ideas. Whatever you do, just get into action so that you can reap the rewards of having the arts as an integral and joyful part of your life.

Chapter 14: Imagine - A Nation of Artists

I began this book by telling you about my decision to quit my railway job and go after my dream of being an artist. At the same time, I decided to fulfill another dream of traveling around the world. I decided to go to Asia and Australia for a year. During that time, I spent four months in Indonesia, mostly in Bali, a small island whose artistic soul beats strong. There, I did an apprenticeship with a master mask-maker and learned how to make masks out of wood.

In Bali, I found there is no rigid line between artist and non-artist. Everyone participates in the arts in one form or another. At one bed and breakfast where I stayed, the man running the place was also a painter. He showed me many paintings he had done of the people and landscapes of Bali.

Ida Bagus Anom, the mask-maker I apprenticed with, not only worked full-time making masks and teaching apprentices, he also was well-known as a dancer and would perform at evening ceremonies and festivals, of which Bali has many.

At another bed and breakfast, the couple who owned the place were also teachers. The wife was a dancer and her husband was a member of a gamelan orchestra.

In Bali, whether a person is a farmer, shopkeeper, traditional healer, or in another occupation, everyone takes part in some form of artistic activity, whether that's singing, dancing, music making, creating sculptures, or batik paintings. Family, work, spiritual life and artistic life are all bound up together and there is no heart-wrenching split between art and daily life.

Here, I found a society where you don't have to make a choice to be an artist and give up everything else. You don't have to be a great genius to pursue an art. It is just assumed that because you are human, art is a part of your life.

Wouldn't it be wonderful if we had the same cultural paradigm here! What would it be like if we just assumed everyone was creative and welcomed them to express their creativity in whatever way it wanted to manifest?

What if we didn't say that we must choose between being a real artist, having financial security and having time for our families? What if we organized our society to allow for this to happen? And what if we didn't subscribe to the notion of the lonely artist in the garret, but instead, embraced a much more communal view of art making? What would that allow us to do or to be?

In the meantime, even though we may not have the capacity as individuals to change our whole society, let's put in motion things that begin the change at a ground level. Let's stop idolizing artists on the one hand and not valuing their services and work on the other.

Let's begin by throwing out all our cultural assumptions that keep us from valuing our artistic souls and following our passions. Let's throw out our assumptions that we have to be great at any art form to justify doing it. Let's throw out the assumptions that we have to do it alone or in a certain place. Let's be just as creative and revolutionary about the assumptions that lie beneath our cultural lives as we are in our artistic expression.

NOTES

[i] Excerpt from "Hieroglyphic Stairway" from Drew Dellinger's *Love Letter to the Milky Way: A Book of Poems* (White Cloud Press, 2011) p.1.

[ii] See Drew Dellinger's website at http://www.drewdellinger.org in the "about" and "reviews" pages. On his website you can also see the "Planetize the Movement" video of Drew reciting his poem, "Hieroglyphic Stairway."

[iii] Dan Berrett, *"The Myth of the Starving Artist,"* Inside Higher ED: May 3, 2011, https://www.insidehighered.com.

[iv] Natalie Goldberg, *Wild Mind: Living the Writer's Life* (Bantam Books, 1990) p.44.

[v] Linda Massarella, "Artist 'steamrolls' into seventh decade," Montreal Daily News, October 15, 1989.

[vi] Interview with Teresa Stratas by Ulla Colgrass in *For the Love of Music: Interviews with Ulla Colgrass* (Oxford University Press, 1988) p.164.

[vii] Barbara Sher, in her book, *Wishcraft: How to Get What You Really Want* (Ballantine Books, 1979) p.136.

[viii] Broken Pencil: The Magazine of Zine Culture and the Independent Arts, Issue 49- Fall, p.22.

Books to Enjoy

These are a few of my large collection of books that have provided me with inspiration and guidance in the joys and challenges of the creative life. They include some more recent discoveries, along with books that I've treasured for years. Enjoy!

ARTS AND CREATIVITY

Rita Mae Brown, *Starting from Scratch*

Julia Cameron, *The Artist's Way*

Mihaly Csikszentmihalyi, *Creativity: Flow and the Psychology of Discovery and Invention*

Nathalie Goldberg, *Wild Mind: Living The Writer's Life*

Nathalie Goldberg, *Writing Down the Bones*

Lyn Le Grice and Christopher Baker, *The Art of Celebration: Creative Ideas for Special Occasions*

Kim Rosen, *Saved by A Poem: The Transformative Power of Words*

OTHER BOOKS

Tony Buzan, *The Ultimate Book of Mind Maps*

Byron Katie and Stephen Mitchell, *Loving What Is: Four Questions That Can Change Your Life*

Rick Carson, *Taming your Gremlin: A Surprisingly Simple Method for Getting Out of Your Own Way*

Timothy Ferriss, *The 4-Hour Workweek*

Jennifer Lee, *The Right-Brain Business Plan*

[95]

Alex Loyd and Ben Johnson, *The Healing Code: 6 Minutes to Heal the Source of Your Health, Success, or Relationship Issue*

Margaret Lobenstine, *The Renaissance Soul: Life Design for People with Too Many Passions to Pick Just One*

Anne McGee-Cooper, *Time Management for Unmanageable People: The Guilt-Free Way to Organize, Energize and Maximize Your Life*

Barbara Sher, *Refuse to Choose!: Use All of Your Interests, Passions and Hobbies to Create the Life and Career of Your Dreams*

Barbara Sher, *Wishcraft: How to Get What You Really Want*

Get your FREE "Jumpstart Your Creative Life Package"

Here's a special gift to help you further on your creative journey. This gift pack contains the "Life Design for Creative Souls with Many Passions Mini-Course" and two audio downloads to inspire and empower you.

You will discover how to:

- get out of the feeling of being overwhelmed and balance your different passions and interests
- cultivate happiness, focus and flow in your everyday life
- eliminate negative money patterns that block abundance in your life

Grab this inspiring FREE package on living your creative passions at: http://thehappywellfedartist.com/gift

For further free resources to help you in your creative life and to find out more about my coaching services and programs, visit http://katiecurtin.com.

Also, be sure to sign up at http://www.creativitycafeonline.com to get access to free interviews with today's creative leaders and innovators.

Please Leave a Review

Find this book inspiring and valuable? I'd be very appreciative if you review it and spread the word, encouraging others to cultivate their artistic gifts and get their projects out in the world!

If you notice any areas for improvement, please email me at contact@katiecurtin.com with your suggestions. If you have experiences that pertain to the topic of the book and would like to be featured in future editions of my book or on my blog, I'd love to hear from you.

Thank you!

Katie

Made in the USA
Lexington, KY
26 June 2015